Sailing  *to the Wind*

Philip Beale
and
Sarah Taylor

The Lulworth Press

First published in Great Britain in 2012

The Lulworth Press
An imprint of LCP
Hampton House
Longfield Road
Leamington Spa CV31 1XB
www.phoenicia.org.uk

Copyright © 2012 Philip Beale

ISBN 978-1-908913-04-3

This book is dedicated to my late mother,
Elizabeth Beale, who set me on the path towards learning about
ancient cultural influences, discovery and adventure.

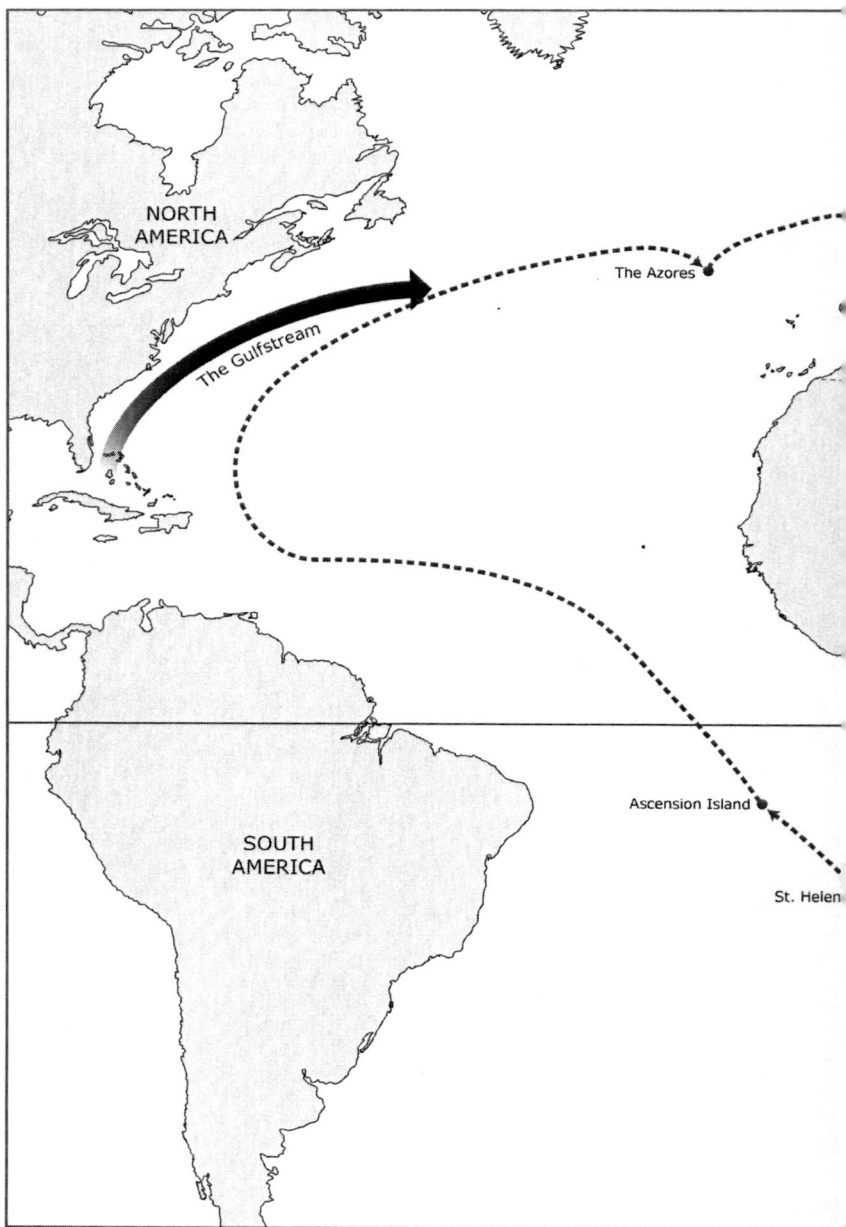

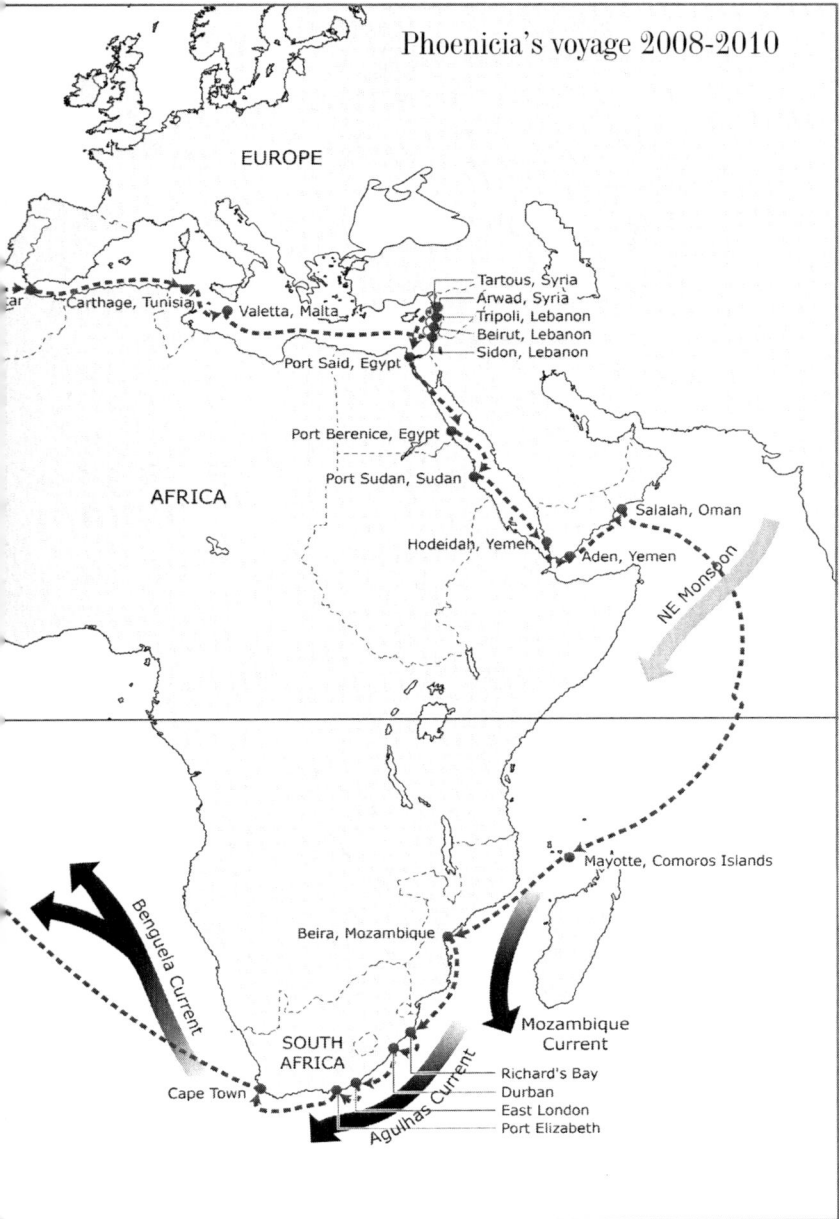

Phoenicia's voyage 2008-2010

EUROPE

Carthage, Tunisia

Valetta, Malta

Tartous, Syria
Arwad, Syria
Tripoli, Lebanon
Beirut, Lebanon
Sidon, Lebanon

Port Said, Egypt

Port Berenice, Egypt

Port Sudan, Sudan

AFRICA

Salalah, Oman

Hodeidah, Yemen
Aden, Yemen

NE Monsoon

Mayotte, Comoros Islands

Benguela Current

Beira, Mozambique

Mozambique
Current

SOUTH
AFRICA

Richard's Bay
Durban
East London
Port Elizabeth

Cape Town

Agulhas Current

PHILIP BEALE was born in England in 1960. He was an officer in the Royal Navy before embarking on a successful City career. In 2003 he left to pursue an ambition to reconstruct an 8th century Indonesian vessel, known as the Borobudur ship, which he sailed 12,000 miles across the Indian Ocean from Jakarta to Ghana. Sailing Close to the Wind is the story of his second historical sailing expedition, as he attempts to uncover the truth behind a Phoenician circumnavigation of Africa. Philip lives in south Dorset, from where he runs Pioneer Expeditions, a specialist adventure travel company. He also devotes his time to motivational speaking, giving presentations and carrying out consultancy work for a wide range of organisations.

SARAH TAYLOR was born in Oxfordshire and lives in London. She has a First-class Honours degree in history, a keen interest in the arts and culture and has travelled extensively. She has followed the Phoenicia project from the outset and this is her first book collaboration.

'Never, never, never give up.'

Winston Churchill

Sailing Close to the Wind

Introduction

For millions of years the oceans lapping Africa's shores have shaped and defined the contours of its coastline. These waters can be hypnotically tranquil then, with little warning, ferocious and unforgiving to those who venture out on them. It is in these oceans, more than two and a half thousand years ago that this story begins, when a fleet of black ships sailed from their 'Purple Empire' into the unknown. Using the sun and stars they navigated a coastline as then unmapped, through some of the world's most treacherous seas, in a circumnavigation of Africa that would take three years to complete. It was this epic journey, lost in the passage of time, that captured my imagination and which, in 2008, I sought to recreate.

It was a huge undertaking: to design and build a ship that was as true to the original as possible, then to organise an expedition to prove her worth. Not content with that, I wanted to captain her on her long and perilous journey. I was driven by the challenge and it appealed to my sense of adventure, but I had never attempted a project as big or as ambitious as this before. All I had in my favour was my capacity for hard work and a steely determination to see it through.

Who were the Phoenicians and what was it about them that fascinated me so much? Although largely forgotten today these were the people who had built King Solomon's temple and commanded his fleet. They had no vast empire to rival the Greeks or Romans; from 1200 to 200 BC the region they occupied was largely confined to parts of modern-day Lebanon, northern Palestine and coastal Syria. Despite being no more than a collection of city states, each retaining their own identity and character, together Tyre, Byblos, Sidon, Beirut and Arwad were renowned, not for their warlike exploits, but for their trading and seafaring skills. Assisted by their alliance with the powerful Egyptian pharaohs that lasted for over a thousand years, their sphere of influence extended far beyond their shores, spreading out into the Atlantic, throughout the Mediterranean and down the Red Sea, from where they traded with India and voyaged to East Africa on the pharaohs' behalf.

Phoenician merchants sold a wide range of goods, in particular a valuable purple dye, a commodity with which their empire became synonymous. They created a glass industry, a wine trade with Western Europe and were quick to recognise the huge wealth they could accrue from the acquisition of silver and other metals. Commerce was able to flourish further as they developed an alphabet, a method of record keeping and a system of general insurance for sharing risks among merchants and ship owners.

However, without the means to take their merchandise further afield, their success would have been limited. It was in the area of maritime development, particularly ship construction, that the Phoenicians excelled. They pioneered new building techniques, which allowed them to create vessels far superior to their rivals. These were known as the 'black ships' as they were coated in pine tar to prevent the dreaded teredo worm from destroying the timbers and to protect the wood from drying out in the hot Mediterranean sun.

When it came to sailing these ships it was the huge advances they had made in the field of astronomy that led to revolutionary change. Their understanding of the night sky allowed them to voyage during the hours of darkness and beyond sight of land using the stars to navigate. As a result even their Greek rivals revered them as 'masters of the seas'. They grew rich and powerful through their seaborne supremacy, their important strategic location between east and west, and their remarkable trading skills. Their sphere of influence extended so far from their homelands that they became one of the world's first global merchants, trading on the three continents of Asia, Africa and Europe.

It is beyond doubt that the Phoenicians were great innovators, hugely successful traders and fearsome sailors, but was it possible they had achieved something much greater than the history books would lead us to believe? Had Bartolomeu Dias been the first to round the Cape of Good Hope in 1488 or Vasco da Gama to circumnavigate Africa a decade later? The more I researched the more I believed the Phoenicians had sailed around the entire coast of Africa two thousand years before these first Portuguese explorers. The only way I could demonstrate this was possible was to recreate a Phoenician ship and put her to the test by making the same journey. I wanted to show they were capable of such an endeavour and restore them to their rightful place in history, but I also had a personal ambition: in trying to prove the Phoenicians could have completed this epic journey I would have to prove I had what it took to complete it too.

Sailing Close to the Wind

1

It doesn't take much for the seeds of an idea to take root and begin to flourish given the right circumstances, a good dose of enthusiasm and determination. It was 2004 and I still felt the thrill of excitement from completing my first expedition earlier in the year. With a fantastic team behind me I had put together a design for an 8th century double outrigger, a vessel I had seen etched into stone on the Borobudur stupa in Java. From this the Borobudur Ship Expedition had been born. After we had built a reconstruction of the ship, we sailed her from Indonesia, around the Cape of Good Hope, to Ghana. I had only intended to demonstrate Asian maritime influence on West Africa but by the time we had arrived in Cape Town the criticism had begun. 'Indonesian Ship A Forgery' ran the headline on the front of the *Cape Times*. The article claimed that the first maritime traders with the African mainland had been Indians. Although I had never claimed the Indonesians had been the first I doubted this theory was true either.

It wasn't until later in the year that I began to look deeper into the question. The more I read the more likely it appeared that the Phoenicians had been the first seafarers to actively trade with Africa. However, when I came across a text by the ancient Greek historian Herodotus, I realised I had stumbled upon a much greater story. Writing a hundred and fifty years after the event, Herodotus claimed that the Phoenicians, sponsored by the Egyptian pharaoh Necho, had circumnavigated Africa in 600 BC. He described a journey travelling from east to west, through the Red Sea and Indian Ocean, returning via the Atlantic to the Mediterranean three years later. One particular passage grabbed my attention:

These men [the sailors] made a statement which I do not myself believe, though others may, that as they sailed on a westerly course round the southern end of Libya [the ancient Greek name for Africa], they had the sun on their right, to northward of them. This is how Libya was first discovered by sea.[1]

Could this have been true? Could the Phoenicians have circumnavigated Africa over two thousand years before the first Europeans successfully rounded the Cape of Good Hope? Herodotus was unable to understand how they could have observed the sun as they described, but it is this piece of information that is crucial. Unless they had made this voyage how would they have known about the position of the sun from the southern hemisphere?

The Phoenicians had gained a reputation as formidable seafarers but this would have involved venturing into an unknown and uncharted world, a hugely difficult and dangerous undertaking. For its time it would have been the equivalent of NASA's first Apollo mission to the moon and, if true, it would completely overturn our knowledge of ancient maritime exploration and rewrite history. The idea of an expedition to test this theory began to take hold in my mind.

A few weeks later the subject came up during a meeting with Professor Barry Cunliffe, Head of Archaeology at Oxford University. We were discussing the Borobudur expedition when I raised the possibility of a new project. He greeted the idea with enthusiasm and offered to introduce me to Jonathan Tubb at the British Museum, a leading expert on the Phoenicians. Jonathan was happy to meet me and intrigued to know how I thought the Phoenicians had achieved a circumnavigation of Africa. I was fascinated with the theory that, sailing from east to west, they would have had to journey out into the Atlantic, following the winds and currents. This would have meant returning to the Mediterranean via the Azores. He was encouraging but reminded me there was no concrete evidence to suggest the Phoenicians had ever reached the Azores. He was right, it was supposition, but the only way to test these assumptions was to reconstruct a Phoenician ship and sail it along the only route I believed they could have taken.

Despite any misgivings, Jonathan was extremely encouraging and suggested some organisations that might be able to help. Most importantly, he gave me valuable practical advice on where to find traditional shipbuilders on the Lebanese and Syrian coasts. In particular he mentioned the island of Arwad in Syria, as on a recent visit he had been impressed with the thriving traditional wooden boatbuilding in progress. Arwad also had the right historical credentials: like Tyre, Sidon, Byblos and Beirut it had once been a Phoenician city, rising to prominence as a major shipping port.

To stand any hope of building a Phoenician ship I knew I needed to carry out extensive research, and to help me with the workload involved I employed an arts graduate called Alice Chutter. She was bright, enthusiastic and seemed to have a genuine interest in what I wanted to achieve. We named it 'Project P' and together we began to collate information on what was known about the construction of Phoenician ships. By an extraordinary coincidence, at around the same time, I met a friend of my father's who was planning a similar expedition. Dougal had spent five years researching Phoenician ships and was intending to build his reconstruction in India. As our ventures were so ambitious I suggested we join forces and we agreed that he should focus on the ship's construction, while I dealt with the organisational side of the expedition.

Six months later we had enough basic information to start looking for a shipwright, and in May 2006 Dougal and I flew to Beirut to explore the Lebanese and Syrian coastline. We met the British Ambassador to Lebanon and, after we had explained what we were aiming to do, he advised us to take the private sector route, as government help would be slow and bureaucratic.

We took note of this warning and avoided government institutions whenever they were mentioned. Although this would limit our options I remained optimistic we could find what we were looking for and I arranged for a driver to take us from Beirut as far south as we could go. Once we had reached the furthest point, a United Nations checkpoint close to the Israeli border, we would turn back and head north along the coast.

Our first stop was Tyre. Today it is one of Lebanon's major ports but ancient history has left its mark alongside the modern city, and beyond the high-rise buildings lie the remains of past civilisations, including the Phoenicians. It was here we found a traditional boatbuilder who had become something of a local celebrity. He had built what is best described as a Phoenician pleasure boat, which took groups of tourists around the harbour in summer. He had trained his two sons to build wooden boats and, as a result, he would neither employ nor teach anyone else these skills in case it took work away from his family. It would take years to build our boat this way and the cost he proposed would far exceed our budget. We thanked him for his time and made our way further north towards Sidon and Byblos.

As we travelled up the coast we found no more than mediocre fishing boats, built with few signs of any great skill or craftsmanship. Despite my disappointment I was beginning to get a feel for these Phoenician cities and the people who had lived in them and it was inspiring me to take the project further. Like Tyre, both Sidon and Byblos had once been thriving centres of industry and trade and at the height of their power, each was renowned for its innovation, enterprise and craftsmanship. Sidon was famous for the manufacture of glass on an enormous scale and with such skill it was considered to be the finest in the world. Along with Tyre it produced and exported one of the most valuable of all their commodities, a purple dye, and to this day Murex Hill stands as a legacy to this industry. It is a mound nearly twice the height of Nelson's column, formed from the discarded shells of murex sea snails, which had been crushed to extract the purple pigment they contained. Ten thousand shells produced just one gram of dye and because of its rarity it was worth more than its weight in gold. It gave me a sense of how the Phoenicians had tirelessly exploited the natural resources around them and how determined and ambitious they had been.

Byblos evoked equally powerful images. It was a city so old that even the Phoenicians regarded it as ancient. The ruins of a Phoenician temple and amphitheatre still remain, and after spending some time at the site I decided to visit the Byblos Museum. As I wandered through the rooms I found a Phoenician stone anchor capable of holding a large ship of the kind we wanted to build. It was triangular in shape and nearly a metre in height. It must have weighed well over two hundred kilograms and would have been extremely difficult to heave up from the seabed. I was getting a sense of the character of these people, how they lived and, most importantly, how they found ways of profiting from the seas around them. They were intelligent, enterprising and highly skilled and I wanted to know how it felt to journey in their wake. However, we still hadn't found a shipwright and we were returning to Beirut empty-handed.

Our only possibility now was in Syria. We took a taxi to the border crossing and made our way over a small piece of no-man's land where we had arranged for a Syrian taxi driver to take us on to Tartous, about thirty-five kilometres up the coast. Our Lebanese driver had refused to take us over the border and, as we discovered later, Syrian drivers would not venture into Lebanon either. The levels of mutual distrust between the two countries are so great that drivers fear they will be picked up by the police or army and accused of spying.

We checked into one of Tartous' hotels and wandered down to the quayside. Across a small stretch of water I could see the island of Arwad, a soft haze of buildings rising out of a deep blue sea. We took a taxi boat for the fifteen-minute crossing and decided to walk around its shores from south to north. As it is less than two kilometres across at its widest point this was a leisurely thirty-minute stroll. Thousands of people inhabit this tiny island and housing is squashed together in a chaotic jumble of one- and two-storey buildings; wherever a space has been found a building has been created. With no traffic to clutter the streets a maze of narrow alleyways has developed, each one leading from the shore and snaking up towards its centre. On the island's northern promontory huge stone blocks, part of what is known as the Phoenician Wall, form an ancient defence against the sea. They are a reminder of its illustrious past, although it was hard to imagine this tiny island once being home to a six-hundred-strong fleet of ships. As we walked we discovered that all around the island, wedged between the houses and the foreshore, were numerous wooden boats at various stages of construction. They were not the smartest boatyards I had ever seen but boats made by skilled craftsmen were being produced, and the place had its own particular charm.

We were keen to learn more about their boatbuilding techniques but neither Dougal nor I spoke Arabic so we planned to hire an interpreter and come back the following day. As we wandered past the shops and small cafés lining the water's edge an old man came out of a restaurant and beckoned us to come and have a drink. He only spoke a few words of English but he told us his name was Mohamad Bakker. When he discovered where we came from he asked us to wait for his son, Orwah, who was out fishing. We were in no particular hurry to leave so we took a seat and ordered a coffee. Half an hour later a young man appeared. As he sauntered in Mohamad took his arm and, with a few words, motioned him towards our table. With a friendly smile and arm outstretched he came over to introduce himself. He was softly spoken and his English was good; it turned out he had been studying in England a few months earlier. After talking about his background our discussion turned to the history of shipbuilding in Arwad. On learning that we wanted to interview some of the boatbuilders, he eagerly agreed to act as our translator.

Over the next two days we conducted countless interviews and drank endless cups of tea with boatbuilders from around the island. With Orwah's help we were able to understand the construction techniques they used, and to our surprise we found that every one of them thought they still made their boats the ancient way, the way the Phoenicians had done. They did not believe us when we told them their construction methods were traditional but not ancient, and that there was a key difference between the two. These boatbuilders first made the frames of their vessels, then nailed the planks to the frames, as European shipbuilders had done since the Middle Ages. The ancient shipwrights started with the keel, building their boats plank first, and only inserting the frames at a later stage. Somewhat perturbed by this suggestion they began to question our interest, so we explained our plan to find a boatyard willing to help us build a reconstruction of a Phoenician ship. Enthusiasm speaks a universal language and it was immediately clear we had come to the right place.

We discussed with them the techniques we wanted to use and the size of the ship we required, but we only needed a single shipwright for the job and one in particular was beginning to stand out. Shipbuilding was in Khalid Hammoud's blood; his family had been building boats in Arwad for generations. His answers were measured and thoughtful, he had the skills we were looking for and, most importantly, I felt that we could trust him. At this stage we had only rudimentary plans but we promised we would be back with a more detailed design later in the year. In the meantime we still had a lot of research to do if we were ever going to get the expedition off the ground.

2

I had no idea at the outset of this project just how unprepared I was and how much work would be involved. In retrospect this was fortunate, as no difficulty seemed too daunting or insurmountable; it was a steep learning curve.

The first problem was finding a ship on which to base our design. I needed to know the details of their construction methods and how they had made their vessels strong enough to withstand the ferocious seas they must have encountered on their journeys. However, no single template appeared to exist and I realised that I had completely underestimated the lack of information on Phoenician ships. We looked at all the available literature on the subject, trawled the Internet for information and wrote to academics in an attempt to find out as much as we could, as well as seeing what we could glean from excavated shipwrecks. Unfortunately, as most vessels of this age had been lying on the seabed for more than two millennia, usually only a few planks and beams had survived. Despite this, each wreck we studied yielded a little more detail on the techniques and materials they had used and, gradually, we began to build up a picture of what a Phoenician vessel must have looked like.

During this extensive research we took a time line from the earliest known vessels, to see how boatbuilding had progressed and changed, then we looked at different regions of the world to discover how traditions had varied. From here we narrowed our focus to ships excavated around the Mediterranean, as boat-building traditions in northern Europe differed from those further south. We already knew that southern craft relied on plank-first or shell-first construction, where planks running along the length of the ship would be butted together to create the shell of the boat, after which the supporting ribs or frames would be inserted. This was the technique I had described to the Arwad boatbuilders.

We discovered that there were two methods to secure these planks together. One was to sew them, which was common practice around the Adriatic and west of the Mediterranean and widespread in other areas of the world such as the Indian Ocean. Locally sourced materials were used for this purpose: in the Middle East and Asia this would have been coconut fibre or coir, whereas in the Mediterranean region it was cotton or linen. The Bon Porté, a wreck found off the coast of St Tropez, gave us a good idea of how this method would have worked. It was thought to be Etruscan in origin and, although poorly preserved, seams sewn with ligatures were still visible. They had been laced through triangular-shaped holes placed diagonally in the plank sides and pegs or fittings would have helped keep them in place. It was one of the processes we replicated when building *Phoenicia*.

The other method of securing the planks was to use mortise and tenon joints. A hole, or mortise, would be made in the plank and a tenon, or peg, would be inserted to secure it. The Uluburun wreck was a much earlier vessel than the one we wanted to recreate but studying it helped us to understand the use of this technique. Dated to around the 14th century BC, it is the oldest cargo vessel ever discovered. It was found off the coast of southern Turkey in 1982 and the type of anchors and the ship's timbers helped to place it in the area we were looking at, possibly even Ugarit or Byblos in Lebanon. This was a very large trading ship, fifteen metres in length with an estimated twenty-tonne capacity and carrying no less than twenty-four stone anchors. It was laden with cargo when it sank, giving up an amazing amount of information on the past. Both raw materials and finished merchandise were recovered including copper, tin, glass, ceramics, jewellery, ivory and even hippopotamus teeth. Most importantly it showed us how the mortise and tenon joints were constructed, how the planks were butted together and how the joints and seams had been sealed with pitch or pine tar to prevent water seepage.

From our research it appeared that the Phoenicians had combined both these construction methods while introducing a new technique, one that the Romans called the 'Phoenician joint'. Once the mortise and tenon was in place it would be locked with two further pins, one placed at each end of the peg. This made the hull much stronger than those of previous ships. Perhaps the Phoenicians felt they had combined the best of both methods or maybe, despite their innovations, they were not fully confident of discarding the practices of the past.

The Ma'agan Michael wreck provided us with a blueprint for how these two styles were combined. Discovered off the coast of Haifa in Israel, it fitted the right time frame, dating to around 500 BC, and from the contents found on board it must have been on a commercial voyage. It was built plank first of pine timber with mortise and tenon joints, but at the stern and stem posts the ship's planks were sewn together with fibres.

As we continued our search for more information, a letter arrived from one of the maritime experts we had contacted. Honor Frost had been a diver for much of her career and was a well-respected maritime archaeologist. In the 1960s she had discovered one of the best-preserved Punic warships ever found, off the west coast of Sicily. Her response to our request for help was enthusiastic and encouraging and she was happy to discuss the project further, so a few weeks later Alice and I travelled to her London home to meet her. Honor turned out to be a delightfully eccentric character and although she was in her late eighties her mind was still brilliantly sharp. Her house was just as fascinating as she was, crammed full of mementoes from a lifetime's maritime adventures. We were shown into a room where bookshelves lined every wall, each one stacked from floor to ceiling with tomes of every size and colour. Lively, animated and totally immersed in her subject, she talked at length about her finds. Suddenly she would think of another fact, jump up, scan her library then clamber onto a stool to reach the exact book she needed to make her point.

We discovered 'my ship', as she called it, was extremely unusual and somewhat of a mystery. This was because Punic warships rarely sank in battle; they would sail unballasted and when attacked they would either break up on the surface or, if they stayed afloat, would be captured by the enemy. This vessel was ballasted, it was newly built when it went down and, from the evidence she had found, it had been launched in a hurry not long after construction. Despite the fact that the Romans copied Phoenician ships during the Punic wars, in all probability this vessel was Phoenician because of the characters found engraved on her timbers. She was discovered a twenty-minute sail from a famous sea battle between the Phoenicians and the Romans, which took place in 241 BC. The Romans had been victorious that day and it had ended the first Punic war. Had this ship been involved in the battle? Other questions also remained unanswered: why had she been so hastily built and launched and where were they trying to get to when she sank?

Most fascinating to me was the evidence of prefabrication. These vessels appeared to have been designed in kit form, producing what was essentially a flat-pack ship. The shipwrights had marked the timbers in various places and guidelines had been painted onto the hull to locate and align the frames when they were placed into the shell. There were some assembly marks on the outside of the hull, usually X or Z shapes, as well as other unexplained marks, what Honor described as talismanic symbols. Having ships partly in kit form would go some way towards explaining how the Phoenicians were able to cross the Nile Delta to reach the Red Sea.

Unfortunately this was a warship, and we knew that a voyage around Africa would have been taken in the more seaworthy merchant galleys, but the principles of construction were similar, despite trading ships being wider to enable them to carry cargo. With an idea of how the hull would have been built, we studied ancient coins, carvings from Egyptian tombs and paintings on ancient Greek vases to understand the rigging and sails. The picture remained incomplete but we decided we had enough information to come up with a design. We found a small company in Dorset that built and repaired wooden boats and they agreed to help. While they prepared the drawings for our ship, we went backwards and forwards delivering pieces of research as we found them. By spring 2006 we had the basis for a design and we sought the opinion of a number of experts to see if we were on the right track.

The first person I turned to was Nick Burningham, an experienced maritime archaeologist, who had designed and overseen the building of a number of ship reconstructions, including *Borobudur*. Although he pointed out a few discrepancies and voiced some misgivings about its accuracy, he was impressed with how far we had progressed. Dr Lucy Blue, Senior Lecturer in Archaelogy at Southampton University, had been carefully pointing us in the right direction since the early stages and suggested we speak to Harry Tzalas, whose name had also come up in conversation with Honor Frost. During the summer of 2006 I flew to Athens to meet him and his colleague, Kostas Damianidis, in the hope that they could help me further.

Harry is a formidable character. He is a marine consultant by profession and is regarded as one of the foremost authorities on Mediterranean maritime archaeology. Persuasive, single-minded, highly knowledgeable and passionate about his work, he had started out by building a papyrus boat in the 1970s. Later he oversaw the reconstruction of a 4th century BC Greek merchant ship known as *Kyrenia*, as well as being instrumental in the construction of the Greek warship *Olympus*, and in having her moved from England to Greece. Kostas had a background in Mediterranean boat design and was now employed by various

Greek museums as an advisor.

Harry and Kostas listened as I outlined the vision I had for my project. When I had finished I presented them with the design we had produced.

Harry looked less than impressed. 'So you want to build a ship in less than a year?' he asked.

I detected a note of incredulity in his voice.

He continued, 'You have severely underestimated the difficulty of building a ship of this construction. We took three years to build *Kyrenia*. What you're attempting to do will be very difficult. You will have to make thousands of Phoenician joints to lock the planks together and that will take time.'

I pointed out that *Borobudur* had the same plank-first construction method and that it had taken six months to build. They remained unconvinced by my optimism or my plan to have her built in Syria, instead suggesting I bring the Syrian shipbuilders to an Athenian boatyard.

Then they turned their attention to the design of the vessel. 'You might as well consign your current design plans to the rubbish bin and start again,' Harry announced.

I was stunned into silence.

'It's all right but it's not accurate enough to be called a Phoenician design. It does nothing to advance our knowledge of ancient vessels and there have been far too many ship reconstructions like that,' and as if he needed to reinforce his point he reeled off a list of names.

It was a crushing blow; months of meticulous research seemed to have evaporated in front of me. I knew that Harry had a point about the design but I was still determined not to let go of my dream and I hoped my disappointment didn't show.

That evening I had a meal with Kostas.

Sensing my dejection he tried to reassure me, 'Harry wants to help you. He certainly doesn't help everyone who comes to him, so don't give up.'

I took heart from this and I was grateful for their time and interest. It had been a setback but despite feeling deflated by his comments I knew it wasn't the end for my project.

The next morning the three of us met again. Harry repeated his concerns, the option of building in Athens and the need to do something that would further our scientific knowledge of the ancient world, but this time he suggested someone who might be able to help me. His name was Professor Patrice Pomey and, although I didn't realise it at the time, he would provide us with the breakthrough we had been looking for.

I had never heard of Professor Pomey before or his work, despite months of researching the subject. He had excavated two wrecks off the coast of Marseilles: the Jules Verne 9 had been conserved and was on display in Marseilles but the details of the other wreck, the Jules Verne 7, which he had been building up over ten years, had never been published. Patrice held all the information at Aix-en-Provence University.

Harry's idea was to see if Patrice would be willing to share his research data and allow us to reconstruct a vessel based on this ship. The JV7 was an ideal match for what we wanted: it was either of Phoenician or Aegean origin and a merchant galley dating from the 5th or 6th century BC. It took several weeks to receive word that Patrice would be willing to meet me to discuss it further. I knew there was no guarantee he would agree to my proposal and there was no particular reason why he should. When we finally met and I told him what I wanted to do it was clear he had reservations, as for him academic study and expeditions did not sit well together. However, despite this he agreed to help and the next day he showed me pieces of the wreck that they had modelled and some of their drawings. We came to an agreement that Kostas would spend a week with Patrice later in the year to record the exact details we needed. This would take the form of a three-part report comprising a design overview, information on the size and spacing of the main timbers and specific details on the joints and fastenings. Each part of the plan would be done in turn and it was agreed that once we had signed off the first part we would not revisit it.

Kostas' work in producing detailed plans was going to be expensive and, not for the last time, I had to use some of my savings to pay for the work, but I had what I needed and construction of the ship could begin.

It was around this time that a letter arrived at the office from another expert. Lionel Casson was a leading specialist in ancient maritime history and he wasted no time in making his point. His letter began:

Dear Mr Beale,

I hasten to write to you to discourage you from undertaking a misdirected project.

He carried on to give his opinion of the ship's diagram we had sent him, which was equally forthright:

There is nothing Phoenician about it, nor can there be, since we have no idea of what a Phoenician seagoing craft looked like.

As for a circumnavigation of Africa he contended that most experts doubted Herodotus' claim:

People throughout antiquity had no idea that Africa extended as far south as it does and subsequent ages were similarly ignorant right up to the Portuguese voyages of exploration around the fifteenth century.

He concluded by suggesting we reconstruct a Portuguese caravel and recreate Bartolomeu Dias' voyage of the 15th century instead. He may have been a leading expert in his field but I refused to believe he was right and the letter was filed away into the project archives.

The work that needed to be carried out on the Jules Vernes 7 took a lot more time than we had originally envisaged. We had hoped to start the building process at the end of 2006 but it became painfully clear that this goal was unrealistic. Reluctantly, I decided to put the project back a year while still working hard to maintain momentum. I knew it was better to take our time and get it right. At least it would give us the opportunity to focus on other important aspects of the expedition. Before we could go any further we needed a team, equipment and sponsorship.

3

'That's another yes,' Alice informed me as she put down the phone and ticked off the final name on the list. With the ship's design coming together we had turned our attention to organising the other aspects of Project P. One of the keys to mounting the expedition was to gather together a group of individuals with the expertise to help advise me on the preparation and management of the ship. Fortunately I knew people with the relevant skills and Alice invited them to be part of a Ship's Committee. The eight-strong team generously gave up their time to help and we arranged to meet every six weeks to check our progress. In return for their assistance they would be entitled to join whichever leg of the journey they chose.

We began compiling a set of requirements and the list was extensive. We needed safety and navigational equipment, a power generator and electrical circuits, not to mention food and medical supplies, each of which had to be researched and sourced. We aimed to get the majority of our equipment in the UK and ship it to Syria at a later date.

The work was divided between the members of the committee, each bringing their own particular experience and knowledge. In Kim Vickers' case this had come from being in the Royal Navy for most of his working life. Hard working and thorough, he took on the task of sourcing numerous pieces of equipment, from outboard engines to the courtesy flags we were obliged to hoist when visiting foreign ports. Once he had found the items we needed he would approach the companies for sponsorships or discounts.

Victoria Sadler's father had run a chandlery business and she had been involved with sailing from an early age. Her connections helped us secure sponsorship for a vital piece of equipment: an integrated chart and wind plotter with depth sounder, radar and GPS. I was also lucky to have made some good contacts during my previous expedition and I managed to obtain life jackets, fire extinguishers and three life rafts from Mark Harriman at Viking Life Saving Equipment. It was this kind of support and sponsorship that was vital to us.

Doug Smith, a good friend and veteran of several other trips, agreed to oversee packing and logistical arrangements. He was a distribution manager and through him we found sponsorship for a container we could use to ship most of our equipment out to Syria. He took on the laborious task of making sure hundreds of items were logged and carefully put away so they could be systematically unpacked and checked off when they arrived. This was to make our lives much easier when enthusiastic Syrian custom officials came to open the container to check its contents.

The fourth member of the committee, Gordon Teenan, was an electrical engineer and project manager by profession. Assisted by Rob Foote, a keen yachtsman whose many skills also included electrical engineering, they had the unenviable task of putting together all the disparate pieces of electrical equipment and working out whether our power generator could cope with the demands we would put on it. We may have been recreating an ancient journey but we were still going to need some very modern equipment and a four-kilowatt diesel generator would lie at the heart of the ship's power supply. It was economical and quiet to run but there was a downside: it was much smaller than other generators on the market, which meant it would be particularly awkward to maintain and service. If anything went wrong we would need the help of an agent to fix it, and while we were at sea for weeks or months at a time we would have no access to this kind of service. It was a chance we would have to take, but one that we paid a high price for later.

For first aid and medical equipment supplies I turned to Reg Hill. I had known him for years and we had sailed together on

Borobudur. He always had a good story to tell, if at times he was prone to more than a little exaggeration. Reg had been involved from the earliest days of planning *Phoenicia* and he was arguably the most experienced member of the committee. He had spent twelve years in the coastguard service, was a seasoned sailor and had participated in organising the Round Britain Race. Added to these skills he was a qualified first-aid instructor and with this knowledge he was able to put together the ship's large medical chest as well as grab bags, which would be needed if we ever had to abandon ship. The work and preparation he put into this task was phenomenal and by the time we left Syria there was very little in the medical line we didn't have on board.

Meanwhile Alice's workload continued to increase as she helped me bring together every element of my plan, and to assist with organisation and logistics I enlisted the skills of a friend and management consultant, Nick Swallow. We were reaching the stage where we needed to raise the profile of the project so we could generate sponsorship, and to enable me do this another friend, Colin Moore, introduced me to Circle, a London-based branding company. For a nominal fee they agreed to work with us on the image we wanted to project. I was keen to promote cultural links between Europe, the Middle East and Africa but at the same time I wanted to get across that this project was about fun and adventure, even though it had a serious historical purpose. By the time we had finished they had helped us produce a logo, brochures and a website. Finally, after much debate we settled on the most obvious choice of name for the ship, *Phoenicia*. Project P now became the Phoenician Ship Expedition.

Paul Docksey, a local graphic designer and artist, carved the figurehead for our newly-named vessel. From a plain piece of oak he created a beautiful and elegant horse's head. It was a striking image and one by which many Phoenician boats were instantly recognisable.

Once I had formalised arrangements with Khalid to build the

ship, I was keen to get official Syrian approval for the project. Alice wrote to the British Syrian Society in London to let them know our plans and received an enthusiastic response along with an invitation to meet the Chairman of the Society, Dr Fawaz Akhras. An eminent heart surgeon and father of Syria's First Lady, Dr Akhras fitted us into his busy schedule. We had a brief but positive meeting, during which he suggested we might want to rephrase some of the points in our brochure so as to appeal more strongly to the Syrian community. This, as far as I could surmise, amounted to saying more about Syria and less about Lebanon.

It transpired, during the course of our conversation, that our expedition had been well timed. Damascus had been chosen as the 2008 Arab Capital of Culture and events and celebrations were going to be taking place throughout the year. The Director of Damascus 2008, Dr Hanan Kassab Hassan, was visiting London the following week and a meeting with her gave me the opportunity to discuss the possibilities of involving the project, and the ship's launch, in the celebrations. Over the next nine months we talked a great deal about such events but, apart from the launch, no other activities ever came to fruition. However, having them as an official sponsor gave the project credibility within Syria, and this enabled us to overcome several serious obstacles in getting the boat built and equipped. Every time we encountered a major problem we would invoke the support of the Damascus 2008 team and, if necessary, ask Dr Hassan to speak to the appropriate people. This could take time but it never failed to work and we were very grateful to the British Syrian Society for this introduction.

Later we wrote to Dr Akhras' daughter, Asma al-Assad, to ask her to become patron of the project but not one of our letters was acknowledged. Although much later she became involved with the launch of the expedition, she was always careful to distance herself from giving us any official endorsement.

During this time *Phoenicia* was gradually taking shape. Nick Burningham and I had arranged to fly out to Arwad every six weeks, alternating our visits to allow us to check progress with Khalid and his team and oversee work on the boat. By this stage we had agreed on the details of the build and had sourced local wood for the construction. It was decided that the keel would be carved from Aleppo pine, the planking from Mediterranean pine, while the ribs would be made from oak and walnut. In addition eight thousand olive-wood pegs needed to be handmade and used to lock the planks together. These timbers were protected and to obtain them we needed a license, but once this had been arranged building work could commence, and in November 2007 the keel was laid. By the New Year the hull was beginning to take shape but there were nine months of hard work ahead until the launch, which was planned to take place in August 2008.

As well as the other work I had given myself I came to one more decision: I wanted to captain my ship. To do this I needed to pass a series of exams to gain an Offshore Yachtmaster's Certificate. I could have saved time, sought an exemption from some exams and taken only those I needed but never one to shy away from a challenge, I pushed myself to do every one. The expedition was a huge responsibility to rest solely on my shoulders so I was keen to have a second-in-command and Reg was the obvious choice. Unfortunately he also wanted to captain *Phoenicia* and he argued I was overstretching myself trying to be both expedition leader and captain. It was an additional pressure but I was determined to prove him wrong and qualify in time.

By the beginning of 2008 the expedition had progressed far enough for me to start the search for crew. I knew we would need a minimum requirement of eight people for each leg; any fewer than that and we would not be able to carry out the basic practicalities involved in sailing a boat like *Phoenicia* for more than a few days at a time. This was because, unlike on modern vessels, tasks such as raising the anchor and hoisting the sail would be physically demanding for those taking part. In the months leading up to this point publicity for the project had been gaining momentum, and articles in newspapers and magazines had begun to appear, along with local TV coverage. This gave us a much higher profile and as enquiries started to come in we began sending out application forms.

We were looking for experience but at the same time we wanted to give opportunities to young people with the right attitude and enthusiasm. This journey could be life changing but there were dangers to be considered and we needed participants to be clear on what an expedition like this would entail, the risks involved and the financial contributions they would need to make. After a day of interviews three candidates who were willing to undertake the entire trip were chosen. Mike Wilcox was an ex-Royal Navy engineering Petty Officer, and the other two, John Bainbridge and Julia Rouse, were students who had recently graduated. Mike seemed full of enthusiasm and energy. He was in his fifties and with years of sailing experience behind him he would be able to make the most practical contribution. John had just completed a degree in international development, was a keen mountaineer and had already participated in a couple of overseas expeditions. He was bright and pleasant and had particularly impressed us. Julia had grown up in Zimbabwe and had recently finished art college. Although she had little travel or sailing experience she seemed keen for a challenge and it was an opportunity for her sketches and drawings to be used to help document the expedition. As the months went by other candidates continued to come forward, both from the UK and abroad, and we were still recruiting in the final weeks before we sailed.

I was keen that this would be a multinational and cross-cultural expedition and for this I wanted Syrian participation, but this was harder to achieve than I had imagined. Unfortunately the practicalities involved in an expedition of this nature deterred any Syrian women from taking part, while many men saw the voyage as too risky and most wanted to be paid. This was out of the question as our crew consisted of volunteers, the majority of whom were making a financial contribution to participate.

However, with only a few weeks to go before we set sail we had a breakthrough when the head of the Federation of Syrian Shipping, Abdul Kader Sabra, came to our aid. He generously gave the project some funds to assist with Syrian participation and this enabled us to start the expedition with three Syrian nationals on board. Amin and Hisham agreed to do the first leg but, as Amin was a medical student at a college in Egypt and Hisham had a legal practice, their commitments would prevent them coming any further. Adnan was in a different situation. He had been a motorboat captain, looking after a motor cruiser for a wealthy Syrian and he seemed very keen to participate. It was only later that we discovered he had an altogether more sinister reason for joining – he was an informant for Syria's secret police and had been relaying every move we made back to the authorities. It was a lesson in the precariousness of our position and the need to tread carefully. One perceived transgression could have ended in disaster for the project.

4

In the months building up to the launch of the expedition the pace of events gathered speed. The long list of equipment we had sourced was now arriving at the expedition's base. This was my office, a converted garage in the grounds of my home in Dorset and it wasn't long before the overflow was piling up in the house. Rooms began to fill with navigational instruments, life rafts and jackets, fire extinguishers and a dozen rolls of the strongest linen canvas for *Phoenicia*'s sails. I took anything I could re-use from the Borobudur expedition, which provided us with anchors, ropes, a storm sail and various navigation lights. In addition we had a generator, several marine batteries, a fridge and a gas oven, complete with piping and fittings, so it would be ready to install when we arrived. Alice and Victoria had gathered together a large collection of utensils and supplies for the galley including pots, pans, cutlery and fifty Ministry of Defence emergency rations. Every piece of equipment was destined for the forty-foot container that would be shipped to Tartous, the nearest mainland port to the island. Although this entailed a great deal of work it was an essential task, as many of these items would have been too expensive, difficult or time-consuming to acquire in Syria. Once in Arwad we would still need to spend precious time installing them onto the ship.

Meanwhile Reg had done such a thorough job in finding medical supplies that we could have almost set up a floating hospital. Unable to acquire morphine, saline drips, oxygen and a defibrillator in the UK we asked the Damascus 2008 Committee if they would help. They put us in touch with the Head of the Tartous Health Authority, who kindly agreed to give us the items we required. Boxes of needles, saline drips and morphine were delivered to us when we arrived and we were told the oxygen and defibrillator would come just before we departed. Regrettably I omitted to mention our gratitude to the Head of the Health Authority in my speech at the expedition launch and he seemed to take offence at this. Subsequently our calls to him were never returned and we left without either piece of equipment on board. This was not a serious loss as later we learned that few boats carry oxygen because of the risks of an explosion and a defibrillator in untrained hands can prove fatal. However, it was a valuable lesson in dealing with the sensitivities involved in giving public speeches, which was particularly the case whenever the First Lady was the guest of honour. The clamour for recognition in her presence was extraordinary. One Syrian who had been helping us with various last-minute items begged me to mention his name in my farewell speech. Unfortunately I had an exhaustive list already and he was another to be severely disappointed.

A few weeks before I left for Syria Doug came down to our Dorset base laden with an assortment of cardboard boxes and rolls of tape, and the container packing got underway. A local farmer allowed us to store all the pallets and boxes in his barn until the following day, when everything was loaded into the container then driven to Southampton dock for onward shipment to Tartous. There was a last-minute rush to get hold of some items, while others never made it to the container. With a few pieces of kit this was because we simply ran out of time, but with more expensive items we would wait as long as possible for sponsorship deals and only at the eleventh hour, if we still drew a blank, would we buy them.

This was the case with the main supplier of satellite airtime, and despite repeated requests for help no support was forthcoming. Finally, we had to turn to the wholesalers who gave us a good deal on a system that would provide us with voice, email and Internet access at trade rates. This was vital for sending blogs and photos back to our website. Unfortunately we made a mistake in specifying our exact requirements for the Raymarine radar equipment, and the unit arrived a couple of days after the container had left. Reg agreed to take both items out as excess baggage, which meant running the gauntlet of customs and security officers, but although we knew these articles would be carefully scrutinised by the Syrian authorities, as they were standard commercial products we were not particularly concerned. As a precaution I asked the Syrian ambassador to London, Dr Sami Khiyami, to advise me on the most expedient way to get our equipment through customs. He arranged for one of the Damascus City of Culture team to meet Reg at the airport, where he would be treated as a VIP guest and taken through a special customs channel. I was assured the whole process would be quick and easy, but the representative failed to turn up and Reg had to go through standard security procedures. On seeing the phone and radar, customs officials immediately confiscated both items and I was summoned to explain why I was trying to bring them into the country. In the meantime I received a call from Dr Hassan, who was incandescent with rage that I had not told her the exact contents of Reg's luggage. Officials appeared to think we had been trying to bring in military equipment and, as Syria's security chiefs were on constant red alert to the threat from Israel, this was viewed as a serious misdemeanour.

I was taken to an army base and led into a small room where I was introduced to a number of military officials; I noticed one of them was a three-star general. We stood around the table and stared at the radar.

'What is it?' one of the officers wanted to know.

I explained its purpose and why we needed it on the ship, but as it differed from radar equipment used on larger vessels, they appeared to think I was lying.

There were some mutterings in Arabic, after which the general intervened. 'Switch it on' he ordered, 'I want to see it working.'

My heart rate quickened, 'I don't think that would be a good idea,' I ventured.

I wondered how he had become a general with that level of ignorance and what the penalty would be for disobeying him.

He fixed me with a penetrating stare. 'Why not?' he demanded.

His reproductive years might have been over but I didn't want mine to end this way so I tried to be as clear as possible, 'If I switch it on it will irradiate everyone in the room,' I replied.

I hoped I had sounded convincing as all eyes turned to the general. After an interminably long pause he nodded his acceptance of my explanation. I tried not to show my relief and willingly agreed to have it inspected once it had been installed on the ship.

There was one more piece of kit to come and although I knew it was pointless trying to get it into the country we still needed it for one of the greatest dangers facing us on our journey around the East African coast. The LRAD, or long-range acoustic device, was a piece of equipment developed for the US military, originally for crowd-control purposes. It could blast out orders, music or warning alarms at fifty times the level comfortable for the human ear. This was our deterrent to Somali pirates operating in the Gulf of Aden and the Indian Ocean and we hoped it would put off all but the most determined hijackers. At the very least I thought it would buy us valuable time while we contacted anti-piracy naval forces deployed in these waters. To avoid Syrian import restrictions I arranged for it to be sent to our agent in Port Said, Egypt, where we would pick it up before making the transit along the Suez Canal.

Once the container had been shipped I could make my own preparations to leave. I had no idea what the next year would bring but I was excited by the challenge and that was enough to eclipse any worries. I flew out to Tartous early in June to wait for the arrival of the crew and to coordinate the fit-out of the ship, but when I arrived in Syria I realised I had some major problems.

I was shocked when I saw *Phoenicia*. It wasn't just that the building work had lapsed even further behind schedule, now it had almost come to a halt. I had not been out for six weeks, although I had been in weekly contact with Orwah. Both he and Nick had been making regular visits and had trusted Khalid's assurances that everything was fine. With Orwah's help I grilled Khalid for answers and eventually got to the heart of the problem: the timber supplies. Instead of buying all the specially licensed wood at once, Khalid had been ordering it in stages, as and when he needed it. Each time he went back to the timber merchants they had to get new authorisation to supply him and after a while they simply refused to provide him with any more. At first Khalid had thought that he could deal with the situation and had played down the issue, but by the time I arrived he had admitted defeat and welcomed any help he could get. I contacted Dr Hassan and explained the situation to her and a bureaucratic game of paper chasing ensued. Official letters had to be signed in Damascus, sent to the Mayor's office in Tartous and finally passed on to the timber suppliers. Eventually the final order started to arrive but two weeks of valuable building time had been lost.

However, this was not the only serious issue. Syrian customs officials in Tartous were refusing to release the contents of our container. I could feel the pressure mounting: we had a ship that was behind schedule, a team on its way to fit it out, and a container with the majority of our supplies and equipment beyond our reach. The harder we tried to resolve the problem the more obstacles seemed to be put in our way. We contacted the agents for the container and a meeting with their customs and logistics expert was arranged. His name was Sacha Hafez and he had been informing us of the problems as they arose, which meant I had no idea if he was part of the problem or the man with the solution.

Doug had already arrived to help unload the container and begin the fit-out of the ship, so he joined me for the meeting. As we were expecting to deal with an officious pen-pusher Sacha turned out to be a pleasant surprise. Not long after entering his office he began to regale us with his love of English football and Manchester United in particular. Uncannily, he had more than a passing resemblance to Eric Cantona. As Doug was a keen Birmingham City fan the common language of football smoothed the way, and the more Sacha learnt about the project the more he wanted to help us. He explained the host of problems we faced: documents for our shipment were not in order, there were taxes to pay and they needed permission to transport the equipment to Arwad. The latter was considered to be a serious issue, which made me wonder how freight ever moved out of the dock.

Sacha assured us that everything could be resolved but, as I was beginning to learn with all these matters, it was going to take time. After a week of waiting, Doug was unable to stay any longer and returned to the UK. It took another three weeks before the container was cleared for opening. By this stage most of the crew had arrived and we had rented a couple of seaside bungalows in Tartous. Late one afternoon we got word that a small commercial boat was on its way with our equipment on board. It came alongside a wharf close to Orwah's house and the entire crew and helpers put their backs into unloading it. By the time we had finished it was after midnight but we had what we needed. Now the race was on to get the ship fitted out in time.

5

The next five weeks leading up to our departure were filled with feverish activity. Often we worked for twelve hours a day, only returning to the mainland to eat and sleep. Even with the intense effort we were putting in, it was going to be a tough challenge to get the ship finished and the conditions were becoming increasingly difficult. From the middle of July temperatures were climbing steadily. The mercury hovered around the mid thirties but the sweltering humidity made it feel much hotter. Many of the crew started work early but with so much to be done we could not avoid the intense heat of the day. Conditions were particularly uncomfortable below deck where Kim, Gordon and Rob were installing the electrical equipment and radar, and Jack, Alice's boyfriend, was hard at work fitting the ship's bunks. One of the most unpleasant tasks was painting the deck and timber with pine tar to protect it from the ferocious heat; aside from the acrid odour it was extremely sticky and, once on your clothes, impossible to remove.

Although the workload was tough most of the crew took to the tasks well and with enthusiasm, but I was concerned to discover cracks appearing in the coherence of the team. Mike and Reg, in particular, became increasingly disillusioned. At first this manifested itself in grumbles and complaints to other crew over the handling of certain tasks. As time went on they would turn up late to breakfast meetings and, regardless of consensus from the others, they would argue for a different way to approach each problem. This cost us precious time and the underlying negativity was damaging to morale. To complicate matters further a personality clash between Reg and Kim was emerging. Both were strong characters and, perhaps naively, I thought that once initial difficulties had been overcome and we had set sail the crew would pull together as one. In the end the question over Reg's suitability for the expedition became an academic one. A few days before our departure, while we were moving the sail, he walked into a concrete pillar and was momentarily knocked unconscious. The pain in his shoulder turned out to be more serious than we had first realised and he returned to the UK suffering from a broken collarbone. He never rejoined the ship, although he gave us help and support via email throughout our journey.

Two more crew had also joined us by this point. Merryn Johnson had recently graduated in Middle Eastern studies and, as she was able to speak Arabic, she had been helping with liaison work in Damascus. Eric Hebert was a professional traveller, white-water rafter and marine engineer. He had considerable experience of sailing tall ships and was to play an invaluable role in overcoming the many challenges we faced in the weeks and months ahead.

Despite the hard work we were putting into the preparations, time was running out so at the end of July we decided to launch *Phoenicia* and complete the fitting-out process once she was in the water. Boat launching practices go back thousands of years and although they vary from culture to culture they are always observed in some shape or form. Khalid made the arrangements and on the morning of the launch we prepared *Phoenicia* by roping her to a small boat, which would pull her down the ramps and into the water. A BBC Cairo television crew had arranged to film the event, and as word of the launch reached the islanders a crowd began to gather by the quayside and in boats around the harbour. To comply with local tradition an imam was invited to perform the ceremony. After he had recited prayers for the ship and her crew, a goat was dispatched on deck, a practice observed throughout the Middle East. With the blessing over, *Phoenicia* gradually edged into the water as the crowd cheered. The local children particularly loved the event, and spent the afternoon shinning up a rope and clambering onto the deck before throwing themselves off into the oily water below. We received good publicity for the expedition, but the departure date was looming and we still had many hours of work to complete.

Our efforts continued at a frantic pace. Weeks had now gone by without a day off for any of the crew, but as the time ebbed away the lists became shorter, as each task was completed and the next one begun. Julia was in charge of provisioning and twelve week's worth of food and supplies found a home on board, including three tonnes of drinking water. As other crew concentrated on their respective tasks the rest got involved with whatever needed to be done, helped by numerous friends who had come out to lend their support.

With the weather window narrowing we decided to get our final official duty out of the way before we began sea trials. We set a date for the departure ceremony and prepared for a big send-off. Support for the project within Syria had been growing as word of the expedition spread, but the arrival of an unexpected visitor a few weeks earlier had raised our profile even further. One morning the First Lady turned up unannounced to see the ship, discuss the project and meet the crew. She was charming and well informed and the excitement her visit generated gave everyone a boost. Once she had shown an interest a large number of Syrian VIPs enthusiastically embraced the idea and many were very generous to us, including Byblos Bank, who agreed to sponsor the departure ceremony, which had been organised by the Damascus 2008 Cultural Committee.

On 11th August *Phoenicia* took pride of place at the end of Arwad's main jetty as a huge crowd of invited guests, islanders, film crews and photographers gathered. A pulse of excitement travelled through the audience as the First Lady arrived, flanked by an entourage of security. Once she had taken her seat and the crew had lined up on deck the ceremony got underway. The crowd fell silent as a woman began to sing, her haunting voice ringing out across the harbour, and as she walked along the jetty, men and women in traditional costumes, their faces painted gold, danced to the music. The pageantry was followed by speeches pledging Syrian support and wishing us well. In turn, I talked about the aims of the project and thanked everyone, or nearly everyone, for their help. With the formalities completed and the First Lady on board we sailed out of the harbour to a great fanfare; twenty minutes later we delivered her to a waiting vessel. Of course, with such an impressive send-off, most people attending thought we were leaving immediately. In order to maintain the charade we sailed off into the night, only to return to Arwad harbour a few hours later.

We had completed our official obligations, but before we could leave we needed to test *Phoenicia*'s seaworthiness. This also allowed the crew a chance to get to grips with the physical demands of sailing her, as with no winches or other modern devices to help them, they would have to use their own strength to pull up the yard and sail, which together weighed a tonne. My original intention was to carry out a month of sea trials, but with so many problems and delays this time frame had shrunk to just a few days. Unfortunately it soon became evident that we had a number of technical problems: the large square sail was far too big, and the tree the mast had been made from was much smaller than the one we had originally specified. This meant the top of the mast was weaker than I had anticipated and we needed to make adjustments to the rigging to strengthen it. With chainsaw in hand, Khalid got to work cutting two metres off the length of the yard. Both the working and ceremonial sails had to be reduced by the same amount, while the canvas was trimmed and painstakingly resewn.

These challenges were time-consuming but they could be overcome with relative ease. The sea trials had revealed a far more serious problem. *Phoenicia* had two huge, oar-like rudders that rested on horizontal beams or thwarts, and it was these quarter rudders that provided the steering mechanism for Phoenician ships. However, when we attempted to turn the ship, we found the water pressure against the rudders was far too great and they would jump away from the thwarts. We had frequent debates over how to resolve this, mistakenly believing the thwarts were too small. We failed to see that we needed additional strong points where the rudder linked to the ship, and instead we built wooden blocks around the thwarts to hold them in place. It was a costly mistake.

Having made the adjustments to the ship, the other crucial issue we had to sort out was how we would get from Arwad to the Red Sea. According to Herodotus it was from here that the Phoenicians would have begun their journey. It is likely they would have built their ships in one of the Phoenician settlements near the Red Sea itself or in the Nile Delta and sailed them as far as they could using the partially constructed Suez Canal. This had been built during Pharaoh Necho's reign, taking a route from the river and out towards the Red Sea. They had come to within twelve kilometres of finishing it, but construction had been halted when the Pharaoh's foreign policy advisers suggested his enemies might use it to attack him. Once out of the water their ships would have been transported overland in pieces and reconstructed on site. To get to the same point, we would need to sail *Phoenicia* to Egypt and through the Suez Canal, but with one square sail and no engine she could only sail downwind. In August the wind was blowing from the wrong direction and we would not be able to make it to our starting point without a tow. With help from the President of the Syrian Federation of Shipping we arranged for a small freighter, with cargo to pick up in Egypt, to take us to the head of the Suez Canal.

On the afternoon of 23rd August *Phoenicia* and her crew waited just outside Arwad harbour for the freighter, *Zafer F,* to come out of Tartous. There were thirteen of us eager to leave, including Alice, Doug and Karen Bowerman, a BBC World camerawoman, all three of whom had arranged to come with us as far as the

Suez Canal to get a feel for life on board. As the freighter came alongside there was an atmosphere of excitement and anticipation, no doubt mixed with some degree of apprehension. We had agreed to be pulled by a long rope so the tension on the line would not be too stressful on *Phoenicia*; she was a wooden ship pegged together using ancient methods of construction and not designed to be towed by a modern commercial vessel. We had the captain's agreement that we would travel at no more than five knots, as any faster risked damaging the ship and pulling some of her key timbers out of place. When the rope was secure the signal was given and *Phoenicia* slowly began to move, but we had not travelled far before the block holding the portside rudder in place broke away from the thwart. The force of the water pushing against the rudder had exposed its weakness immediately. My heart sank; our plan to keep it together had failed already. We would have to rely on a single starboard rudder until we got to Egypt and once in port we would have to tackle the problem again.

It took an uncomfortable three days to travel the four hundred miles to the head of the Suez Canal. The constant pounding going into the waves was not a natural sailing motion and, as a result, a number of the crew suffered from seasickness. Despite this we began to get to grips with life on board, with everyone taking turns pumping out the bilges and preparing food. Although under tow, we kept a bow watch and there was always one of us at the helm, making sure there was never too much pressure on the remaining rudder.

It was late into the third night when we arrived at our anchorage point. From here we would wait for a tow to take us the last few miles to Port Faoud, at the entrance to the Canal. We soon discovered that we were positioned at the corner of two merging shipping lanes and the bow watch quickly changed to a lookout fore and aft. The wake of passing cargo ships would rock the boat roughly, sending anything that had not been stowed away crashing to the floor, but at least the rolling motion was an improvement on the tense and forceful pull from the freighter. The following morning the crew took the opportunity to relax and, while some recovered from their seasickness, others cooled down with swimming races and diving competitions. By the afternoon there was still no sign of our tow to Port Faoud so we contacted the agent at the port, only to be told we were too far out for them to reach us. For the first time *Phoenicia* set sail as we travelled the last few miles to the meeting point.

We were towed to a small yacht club in Port Faoud, close to the entrance to the Canal, where we would wait until we were given permission to transit. As Alice, Doug and Karen made plans to return to the UK, Amin and Hisham came to tell me that they had had enough and wanted to leave too. I tried to persuade them to stay but they were adamant; they had found the ship under tow a particularly stressful experience and the thought of being out at sea was too much for them to contemplate. The crew had shrunk by five.

While in port I turned my attention to mending the rudder. Port Faoud would once have been an impressive colonial harbour, but its heyday had long since gone. Now it was faded and shabby and only used by a handful of yachts waiting for permission to enter the Canal. It was a shame that some unscrupulous individuals working at the port saw our arrival as an opportunity to line their pockets. Suddenly a simple block of wood became a precious commodity, for which they wanted to charge us six hundred dollars. Even basic food items had mystifyingly high price tags. Luckily the main town of Port Said was only a short ferry ride away and furnished us with much of what we needed. Once we had secured the rudder block in place we were keen to leave, but the days came and went and nothing appeared to be happening.

Our delay hinged on our need to be assessed by the Port Authorities. Most vessels entering the Canal have to travel in a convoy at a regulated speed and small boats, being much slower than the tankers and cargo ships, have to be checked over before being granted permission to go further. With no engine we would need a tow to stay at a steady speed and for this an engineer had to determine what type of tug we required. We had expected this to take two or three days, but after nearly a week had gone by and no one had appeared I demanded to see the engineer. Although the meeting went well the promised survey team never arrived and the situation was rapidly becoming farcical. We began to fear that we would be stuck in Port Faoud for weeks so I arranged to meet the Chairman of the Suez Canal Authority while asking the Syrian ambassador, Dr Sami Khiyami, if he would talk to him. In true diplomatic style Dr Sami launched a charm offensive with the Chairman. After telling him how much Syria and Egypt had in common, mentioning his mother was Egyptian for good measure, he sought assurance of a safe passage for our historic mission. Meanwhile a number of the crew and I went to the headquarters of the Port Authority, but by the time we arrived we were told permission had already been granted. A day later our tow appeared.

6

inally, a week after arriving in Port Faoud, we began our journey south. At four in the morning a tug from the Suez Canal Authority pulled up next to us and lashed herself to *Phoenicia*'s side. It was a risk being towed again and the strength of such a powerful tug against *Phoenicia*'s wooden hull made her creak and groan, as if she was complaining of the indignity of her lot. I had assumed we would be part of a convoy, but being rafted alongside a Port Authority vessel seemed to give us an independence to take it at our own pace. Throughout our transit we continued at a steady four knots, with boats passing us from both directions. The flat water of the Canal spared the crew another uncomfortably jarring journey but it was noisy and smoke billowed from the tug's exhaust, enveloping us every time the wind changed direction.

As dawn broke the sun's light gave us a clear look at one of the busiest waterways in the world. Although a vital artery for trade, and dominated by huge container ships and oil tankers, it was surprisingly narrow in parts. Once out of the built-up area of the port much of the journey was desert, the white sand peppered with patches of green vegetation, while military installations and lookouts dotted the landscape at regular intervals. During our journey we passed a couple of ships languishing by the water's edge. They had been bombed and left to decay and rust, poignant reminders of the conflicts that have blighted the history of Egypt and Israel. We travelled under bridges and past slipways, used for the ferries that crossed the canal at regular points. At one stage the water opened out into a huge lake before narrowing again. With no need for lookouts the crew spent the day reading, sleeping or recording the journey through photos and drawings. It was much more difficult for me to relax, as every time the tug turned slightly *Phoenicia* would register her disapproval. It was during one of these turns that Merryn spotted a streak of light in the cabin when a plank briefly came away from the rib before closing again. I was becoming concerned we would be pulled apart but, despite the strain on *Phoenicia's* hull, by nine o'clock that evening we emerged unscathed. The hundred-mile journey had taken a tense sixteen hours to complete.

We were taken to a mooring point just south of the Canal, but as we dropped anchor there was a moment of confusion when our tow delayed casting off from us. This left the entire weight of both *Phoenicia* and the tug on our anchor, and as it dug itself into the seabed our anchor chain tightened. By now a strong wind had begun to blow and we made preparations to get some sleep while two of the crew stayed on watch. It was important we got some rest as the following morning we would begin our first proper day of sailing. I was looking forward to the challenge, but there was so much we didn't know and I was still getting a feel for this ship. There was a question mark over her rudders and I wasn't sure how the modified mast and sail would perform in strong winds. I had resurrected a ship from the obscurity of history and her first test was to sail thousands of miles through some of the most dangerous seas in the world. I wondered if she would be able to handle the conditions she would have to endure.

At dawn we prepared to leave. We hoisted the yard then it was all hands on deck to raise the anchor. We put our collective weight behind each pull but it had become too deeply entrenched in the mud the night before and it was impossible to move. After ten minutes of heaving without success, and as I contemplated having to cut the chain loose just to get going, a small pilot boat appeared. We waved the captain over and once he understood our predicament he threw us a line so he could pull *Phoenicia* in the direction of the anchor chain. This allowed us to recover the slack and pull up the anchor, but as the chain began to emerge from the sea we were horrified to discover that ten of the links had burst apart. We had been barely hanging on all night and at any time the ship could have been cast off into the dark, giving us no chance to prepare. Through sheer good luck we had escaped such a potentially dangerous emergency. We thanked the crew of the pilot vessel and threw them a carton of cigarettes.

Once we had let off the brailing lines the sail unfurled from the yard and we began our journey south down the Gulf of Suez, passing the tankers waiting for their chance to join a convoy heading north. During the morning the sailing was good and we were able to keep a steady pace, but as the afternoon progressed the winds gradually started to pick up. We reduced our speed by furling the sail but they continued to gather strength. As they reached twenty-five knots the sail began to pull higher and higher up the mast. Suddenly the wind changed direction, the sail was backed and all hell broke loose. The gusts swirled behind the canvas, twisting it awkwardly around the mast, and a brailing line came free, hitting Julia squarely in the face. Although shocked she was unhurt and our attention rapidly switched to the yard, which had begun slamming furiously against the mast. We managed to get it down quickly, but almost immediately *Phoenicia* turned beam onto the sea and the waves began striking her from the side. With the force of the water pounding against the ship the port rudder jumped out of its socket. Despite the conditions, we had to get the rudder, weighing close to four hundred kilograms, out of the water. It took most of the crew and a back-breaking effort to pull it on board. Without the sail and with our angle to the waves we were rolling violently and to get her back under control I needed the sea anchor, a large marine parachute. We hauled it to the stern, threw it into the water and watched as the attached ropes rapidly uncoiled and shot out across the side. The canvas opened up behind us, like a giant squid with outstretched tentacles. In the chaos we had no idea that one of the anchor ropes had got caught on a port rail post. The strength of the winds and *Phoenicia*'s weight created such a force that the post had almost broken in half.

Phoenicia had stopped rolling but our problems were far from over. Shortly afterwards the wooden block that held the other rudder in place broke free and for the second time we had the exhausting task of hauling in this heavy weight. Now we were without sail or steerage and drifting down the Gulf of Suez. I issued a warning over the VHF to other vessels in the nearby shipping lane that we were 'Not Under Command' and unable to manoeuvre. Not a single vessel replied and it wasn't until some hours later that we realised the radio aerial had accidentally been pulled out during the evening's dramatic events. Fortunately I had sent a copy of the warning to our security agents requesting they forward it to the UK Maritime Control Centre in Falmouth. In turn, they contacted the Egyptian Coast Guard.

A quick look at the chart showed us we only had about five or six hours before we would be on the rocks, but there was another more immediate problem: there were two oil platforms within a five-mile radius of us. As dawn broke we passed one of them but we were on a constant bearing with the second. If we couldn't gain some sort of control we were set on a collision course and we would have to abandon ship and use the life rafts. I considered the cost of damaging an oil platform, not to mention the humiliation I would feel. More crucially the safety of the crew and the ship were in my hands. I put these thoughts out of my mind and concentrated on what we could do to prevent it happening.

I needed to consult with an experienced head so I woke Kim who was getting some sleep on deck. After a brief discussion I asked him if he thought there was anything we could do to avoid a collision. We had already tried tying a metal bucket to our port side but it had made no difference to our course.

'I just don't know what to do Philip,' was Kim's initial response.

This was not the answer I wanted, and for a minute we were both silent as we contemplated the gravity of the situation.

Then Kim tentatively offered a suggestion. 'How about hoisting the sail slightly to see if we can get some more momentum?'

I had no better ideas and by now we were only a mile and a half from the platform and getting closer all the time. I gave the order, the crew hoisted the yard to a metre above the deck, and we watched as a small section of sail began to billow out. Almost imperceptibly, our course began to change. In the end we passed the oil platform with half a mile to spare. The sense of relief among the crew was palpable, but although we had got out of one predicament we still had little control over the ship. By this stage other vessels in the area knew of our situation and a huge tug, the *Ocean Aswan*, came to our assistance.

Discussions began over the possibility of a tow. Adnan, our remaining Syrian crew member, explained the project to them in Arabic, but the captain needed to check how much the ship's owners in Alexandria wanted to charge. I was dreading the answer, knowing a tow could cost thousands of dollars, but it turned out my worries were unfounded. In an incredible act of kindness they decided to put their tug and ten-man crew at our disposal for half a day free of charge. Now we could get to a safe place, take stock and make repairs to our wayward rudders.

Ocean Aswan towed us for nearly twenty miles, on what was a rough and uncomfortable journey, as we headed into the wind and the waves. Just after dark they left us at a cove off Ras Abu Zanimah, along the Egyptian coast. Relieved and grateful, we even managed to laugh when the tug captain suggested we use our engine to manoeuvre to the best anchor position. As they disappeared into the night we made a quick supper and organised an anchor watch, while the remaining crew tried to get some sleep.

The next morning, as the sun's light spread over the small cove, we reviewed the damage. The locals were intrigued by our arrival and we managed to find one who was able to strengthen the steel bands holding the rudders in place. Meanwhile we made a number of other repairs and replacements to the shrouds and stays. Kim and Mike were sceptical about the quality of the work that had been done on the rudders, but we had little choice and all we could do was hope they would hold. Thirty-six hours later we prepared to leave. Again we had difficulty dragging the anchors out of the mud but eventually, using the power of the hoisted sail, we were able to pull them free.

We left the cove and sailed back out into the Red Sea. Our progress was frustratingly slow and we were becalmed for several hours, although this gave us an opportunity to enjoy the incredible wonders of nature around us. During the afternoon the air filled with the whirring of thousands of wings and the sky turned white as a large flock of storks passed above our heads on their migration south. In the waters below, *Phoenicia* had attracted the curiosity of a large dorado, its vibrant blue scales flashing in the sunlight as it effortlessly glided through the water beside us. Julia wanted to paint it while the rest of us would have preferred to eat it. As we hadn't managed to catch any fish so far it was never in much danger and it soon disappeared. Later we were joined by a small pod of dolphins that playfully weaved through the water, as if challenging us to a race. It was a welcome distraction for an exhausted crew, but serious concerns over *Phoenicia*'s rudders still weighed heavily on my mind.

My fears were realised a few days later when both rudders failed again and we were forced to pull them on board and deploy the sea anchor for a second time. The effort sapped both the energy and the enthusiasm of the crew. The journey so far had been more physically and mentally challenging than any of us could have imagined. Everyone was tired and Adnan was suffering from such bad seasickness that he had taken to lying on the deck, refusing any sort of medicine. At this point I called the crew together for a debate over what to do next. I still thought there were options we could try but Kim's patience had run out.

'We can't go on like this Philip, we have to turn back,' he announced.

There was silence. No one else wanted to speak up, even though I knew there were some on board keen to try again. I kept quiet in spite of the fact I had another plan to make it work. In hindsight I should have handled the situation differently and taken more control, but I was still finding my feet and I didn't feel confident enough in the ship or myself to enforce my point of view.

As I hesitated Kim made his point more forcefully, 'I think we have a morale problem on this ship and we need to pack it in now.'

Our journey had been blighted by problems and everyone was exhausted. Admitting defeat was humiliating, but I realised this was only going to work with a fully united crew.

The sole decision now was to which port we should try to head. Being in the middle of the Red Sea both the Egyptian and the Saudi Arabian coasts were possibilities, but we needed to consider the departure and arrival of crew and the need for medical care for Adnan. After several emails and discussions with Nick Swallow and Alice in the UK, we opted for Egypt. To get there we would need another tow so I contacted the Egyptian navy. They agreed to help but for a fee of twenty thousand dollars; they knew that in our position we had very few options open to us, as it would be impossible to get there under sail. Once I had agreed, an Egyptian patrol vessel was with us within a matter of hours. We braced ourselves for another tow, and this time we knew it would be fifty miles before we reached the nearest port.

7

We arrived at Ras Banas, or Port Berenice, on 17th September, only twelve days since we had set sail from the Suez Canal. It was early in the morning but it was already searingly hot and we soon discovered we were in the middle of nowhere. This was Egypt's most southerly naval base, just a stone's throw from their disputed border with Sudan, and apart from a few military huts and storage tanks there was nothing but desert and distant hills. Our enquiries established that the nearest town was a hundred and fifty kilometres away, not that it would have mattered how far it was as we were promptly told we would not be allowed to leave the jetty, let alone the base. Port Berenice was not an official port of entry and, as a result, they were unable to issue us with entry permits or visas. Eric's hopes of visiting the Aswan Dam were dashed and over the following weeks we found ourselves increasingly mired in red tape and bureaucracy. Virtually every request we put forward was denied with what became a painfully familiar phrase, 'that is not within military regulations'.

This left me with a number of challenges, both in repairing the ship and dealing with the crew situation. For those who wanted to leave, and there were more than I had anticipated, there would be no opportunity for a quick exit and the atmosphere on board was tense. Kim and Merryn had given up as much time as they could, but it soon became clear others would be joining them. Once in port we immediately sought medical help for Adnan. He had been refusing to drink enough fluids and by this stage he was badly dehydrated. With injections and rehydration salts he recovered quickly but he decided to return home. My disappointment was tempered with relief, as his seasickness may have become much more of a problem later and a medical emergency in the middle of the Indian Ocean would have been a disaster.

Some packed their kit as they waited for permission to disembark but so little progress was made over the first few days that tensions rose to boiling point at times. It was hot and oppressive, we couldn't leave the confines of the ship and for those who wished to quit, *Phoenicia* had become a floating prison. At one of our daily meetings to discuss how we could make progress, frustrations came to a head.

'For God's sake Philip, we're not immortal,' Julia blurted out during one particularly heated exchange.

Suddenly it was clear how frightening the last few days had been for her. She had experienced as much adventure as she could take and it came as no surprise when shortly afterwards she decided to head to Cairo with Merryn. There were others who had reached their limits too.

Mike came to talk to me the first morning of our arrival, 'I just can't do this anymore. I need a rest,' he confessed.

I had overestimated his stamina and now I was losing two of my core crew. Fortunately Eric and John were still keen to carry on and the expedition had become such an all-consuming passion for me that I never contemplated giving up. However, I could see the situation deteriorating further if we didn't make better progress so I asked Merryn, who spoke Arabic, to coordinate the arrangements for the crew members who were leaving. The Egyptian naval officers seemed quite taken with her and were only too happy to help. Over the following days forms were filled in, official papers were stamped and five relieved crew said goodbye and left the ship.

Once they had gone I could concentrate on finding someone to repair *Phoenicia*, particularly her rudders; if we couldn't get her fixed the expedition would be over. I discussed the options with our naval contact, Captain Ayman, and he suggested we speak to an ex-naval officer who ran a hotel in Hurghada, several hundred kilometres to the north. It was hard to see how he could be much use, or why he would want to come such a distance south to help us, and I declined the offer, convinced I had a better idea. I had noticed that alongside the naval base at Port Berenice there was a small fishing fleet and a few processing sheds. I asked Captain Ayman to find out if one of the carpenters who worked there would be able to help us, and a couple of days later a slight, swarthy looking individual arrived to cast his eye over the damage. He agreed the work could be done for a hundred dollars before he scurried away, assuring us he would be back later. It seemed rather cheap and when a few days went by with no word from the carpenter I asked Captain Ayman what had happened. He shook his head disapprovingly while telling me he had never trusted him. He thought it unlikely we would ever see him again.

We were back to square one and our only option now was the hotel manager in Hurghada. We made contact with little hope of success but to our great surprise a carpenter arrived within a couple of days. He agreed to fix the spare yard across the deck so it would support the quarter rudders, making them less likely to jump out of their sockets whenever there was great tension under sail. He went back to Hurghada, promising to return when he had picked up some supplies. At the same time we asked the Egyptian navy if they could make some steel safety bands to attach to the lower thwart. We added a new thwart above this one so the whole rudder housing would be much more secure, or at least secure enough to get the ship down to Port Sudan. Once there we would add a third thwart above the deck on the railings so that each rudder would have three support points. We knew if that wasn't going to hold them in place then nothing would.

With only three of us left our daily meetings took on a new significance and it became an important way for us to stay focused and positive. Morale remained high, although for one disgruntled parent our journey had become too much to take. John's father had called the office, furious at what he thought was a lack of regard for the dangers we faced. He was so angry he threatened to report the expedition to the Royal Geographical Society, one of our supporters. Nick Swallow called him to explain the extreme lengths we had gone to in assessing the risks and the many precautions we had taken. Eventually, with his anxieties assuaged, he backed down but John was unimpressed when he discovered what had happened.

'I wish he wouldn't interfere,' he told me with a despairing shake of his head. 'This is my project and I can make my own decisions.'

John was new to sailing but he had taken the journey and our difficulties in his stride, rarely expressing concerns about what lay ahead. He would help with any task and, being agile and slight with great climbing skills, he was more than willing to scale the mast whenever needed. I was relieved that he had decided to stay with the expedition.

While we waited we spent much of our time carrying out other repairs, resizing the shrouds and cleaning the ship. By the time we left we had almost re-caulked the entire deck twice. When our first experiment with a chalk cement failed we replaced it with a thick gooey mixture of pine tar and chalk, a discovery we were sure the Phoenicians must have made. The rest of the time we spent reading and playing cards. The only certainty we could rely on from shore were deliveries of fresh food. We discovered that if we placed an order in time supplies would arrive on a weekly truck from the Egyptian Naval HQ in Alexandria, just over three thousand kilometres to the north. Although our first order took a week to arrive, the fresh fruit, vegetables and other items on our list did much to lift our spirits.

However, we still faced a major challenge: we needed to find more people to join the ship. Believing we had recruited most of the core crew this was not a problem we had anticipated. Alice, who was running the UK office, hit on the idea of advertising for recruits on some sailing and crew-finding websites. This produced a couple of interesting candidates.

Our first response was from Jev Maksimovs, a Russian living in Latvia. He had thirty years experience as a merchant seaman and had a passion for travelling and recreational sailing. At the time he heard about the expedition he was in Spain and made plans to fly to Cairo to join us. The Egyptian navy had already warned us that it would be difficult for him to get to the naval base without their authorisation and help so we were both surprised and impressed when one morning he calmly walked onto the ship. He had hitched a lift down the coast to the base where they had let him in without any difficulty. It was great news, but even with Jev we still needed another two crew to take us to six and this number would only allow us to sail for short periods of up to a week.

I turned my attention to finding any friends or supporters who would be prepared to join us for this stage of the journey. It was a relatively short hop of a few hundred miles to Port Sudan, but finding volunteers was complicated even further due to the nature of the next leg. Sailing in the southern part of the Red Sea towards the Gulf of Aden put us at risk of piracy, which was enough to deter most prospective crew. Despite this I started sending emails to as many trusted friends as I could, in the hope that some of them would volunteer. There was no doubt I was offering them an experience of a lifetime, unfortunately it was not a particularly appealing one. We were in the middle of nowhere, on a ship with no engine, and we were about to sail into waters notorious for piracy. No wonder most declined. They were too polite to say so but many must have questioned my sanity by this stage. My options were running out but just as I was wondering what to do next, I made a breakthrough. Rebecca Delmar-Morgan, an old friend, who was also an adventurous traveller and a keen sailor, expressed a wish to come out. Shortly afterwards Nick Swallow, the project's chairman and Jo Phillips our PR adviser, agreed to join us. The situation was starting to look a little brighter.

This solved my immediate problem, but I needed to find crew to participate in the entire trip. I decided that my best option was to try to contact some of the Indonesians who had been with me on the Borobudur Ship expedition; with impressive sailing experience and an appetite for adventure they would be perfect crew. In particular I was keen to get in touch with Sulhan, Aziz and Sudirman, known as Dirman to his friends.

Getting hold of Sulhan and Dirman was a complicated process as both lived on a small island over ninety kilometres north of Bali. Communications with the island were difficult at the best of times, but through a friend I managed to contact a shipbuilder who lived on the mainland, and he agreed to get in touch with them for me. This indirect way of making all the arrangements would take time with no guarantee of success. Unfortunately it wasn't until many months later that Dirman was able to join us.

Aziz was in a different situation. He was a Jakarta-based journalist and photographer and could drop everything at virtually a moment's notice. He was passionate about expeditions and foreign travel and needed no encouragement to join us, so we organised his flight to Egypt. As he would be joining the ship we never considered he would have a problem getting entry into the country, but when he arrived he was detained at Cairo airport. He was allowed to call me only once to explain what had happened and I was unable to contact him again. I tried to get the Egyptian navy to speak to immigration officers in Cairo but they refused to get involved. By now Merryn was back in the city but she had no luck trying to contact the airport officials either.

In the meantime, Egyptian immigration officers were becoming increasingly aggressive with Aziz and what started as verbal abuse and bullying soon turned to violence. After three days of detention they tried to force him to sign a piece of paper making him agree to pay for the cost of a return flight to Indonesia. By now Nick had arrived in Cairo and had managed to track down the immigration officers concerned, only to learn that Aziz had just been deported. He had been given one of the last seats on a flight to Jakarta and we were informed that we owed Etihad Airlines fifteen hundred pounds for his ticket. Aziz was back in Jakarta and understandably shaken by his experience so I turned to close friends, Lily Wardono and Farquhar Stirling, who lived there to see if they could help sort out the mess. They successfully managed to smooth the way with the airline, who agreed to help get Aziz and the two other Indonesians on a plane to Port Sudan, our next port of call.

By this stage Nick, Jo and Rebecca had met up in Cairo and, having heard that repairs to the ship had not been completed, they waited in Hurghada until they knew we were ready to leave. Unfortunately during this time Jo got a message to say her mother had fallen ill, and she had to return to England. We were down to the bare minimum of six. We would be fully stretched and the first test was to come sooner than I thought.

With rudder repairs completed and our new crew gathered we prepared to leave. Unusually high winds on the day of our departure delayed us until early afternoon, but eventually we said goodbye to the navy personnel who had come to wave us off and set sail. We were relieved to be on our way again, but our buoyant mood was short-lived. Despite having the wind behind the sail, the weight of the ship and the strength of the wind seemed to set *Phoenicia* on her own path and she refused to turn in the direction we were steering her. Instead, she rounded up into the wind and within a few minutes she was heading across the bay, in full view of the Egyptian navy. Embarrassment was the least of our problems, as by now we were heading towards the treacherous reefs that ran along one side of the bay.

Immediately the entire crew sprang into action. Rebecca leaned as hard as she could on the rudderpost, while Eric took the tender to try to nudge the boat around. Nick had made his way to the bow and began shouting back a commentary on our distance from the rocks. For the next twenty minutes I stood at the helm willing her to start to turn, but it was as if she had set her mind on her own course, and like a disobedient child was refusing to listen. No amount of coaxing or cajoling was going to persuade her.

For a brief moment I thought we might just edge past the reefs, then I heard the heightened urgency in Nick's voice, 'We're getting closer, a hundred metres … fifty … forty … we're not coming round, we're not going to make it.'

A frenzy of activity followed as we rushed to get the sail lowered, but the halyard had jammed and it was impossible to move. There was only one option left. I released the anchor and as it dropped out of sight the heavy chain rapidly unravelled and disappeared into the water after it. As the attached rope pulled taut *Phoenicia* groaned to a sudden halt. I felt sick as I looked at our position. We had stopped ten metres from a line of razor-sharp rocks that would have sliced through *Phoenicia*'s hull like a knife and ended the expedition in a humiliating disaster.

We were out of immediate danger, but now we had to work out how to extricate ourselves from our predicament. A couple of fishing boats nearby had watched the drama unfold but must have decided this was solely a spectator sport, so I sent a radio message back to the Egyptian navy. A little later a couple of boats arrived and, sensing the opportunity for a profit, their captains lost no time in getting down to business. I suggested a price, which was met with a display of disapproving expressions, and we started again. Eventually we came to an agreement and we prepared to be towed.

It took several hours to be pulled past the reefs, through the port mouth and out into the main shipping route beyond. Once out it was good to be under sail again but the first twenty four hours were tough. High winds and the bare minimum of crew made it hard work. We continued to use the storm sail, as with the mainsail weighing a tonne it was too heavy for us to manage. Two crew were needed on the rudders to keep us on course, which left only four of us to navigate, man the bilge pumps, trim the sails and prepare meals. As a result no one had much sleep initially. Exhaustion aside, much to my relief we were working well as a team. Jev was suffering from terrible seasickness, but he was a tough character and I watched him fight against it and carry on. He was tall, wiry and strong and had no trouble with the physical demands of sailing *Phoenicia*. Once out at sea it soon became apparent that he also had a talent for navigation.

As we made our way along the Sudanese coast the winds began to die back, and once sailing had become easier we were able to get into a rhythm and focus on maintaining our course. The mood remained upbeat and both sail and rudders were work-ing without a problem, allowing us to make good progress at a consistent four knots. Unfortunately thirty miles from Port Su-dan the wind dropped to almost a whisper and *Phoenicia*'s speed slowed to less than a knot. We were frustratingly close to our destination but there was nothing we could do until the winds picked up again. This gave me more than enough time to con-template our approach to Port Sudan, where I knew I would have to negotiate my way past the reefs that lined the approach channels. It was sobering to think that the Phoenicians would have had to do this without any prior knowledge of what they would encounter. As we waited we noticed a flurry of activity in the air above us, and a few minutes later a small bird landed on our bow. A swallow had found a place to rest as it made its ardu-ous migration south. During the day a steady flow of tired birds alighted on the ship, forced to find somewhere to break their journey. Sadly most died from exhaustion but I was struck by their unwavering determination, which pushed them to journey such vast distances and took them to the limits of their endur-ance. We had a long and potentially dangerous voyage ahead but I had the choice to stop and turn back. It made me wonder how much I would risk in the pursuit of my dream.

The following day the winds changed and we were able to sail right up to the edge of the port area without incident. The three hundred miles from Port Berenice to Port Sudan had taken five days. *Phoenicia* had shown her true capabilities for the first time.

9

A long, narrow channel took us past Port Sudan's commercial dock, and as we sailed by one of the cargo ships their crew gave us an enthusiastic cheer. We reached a small harbour where we tied up alongside a few private boats and began to take in our surroundings. It appeared to be a quiet and rather modest place and although the British had established the town as a seaport in 1905, passenger services had long since ceased. Now only cargo ships, many bringing aid to Darfour, and a few private vessels ventured this way. Our main priority was to get *Phoenicia* repaired, but we were keen to use the opportunity to explore what we knew lay beyond our immediate surroundings.

The Arabs gave Sudan the name *Bilad al-Sudan,* meaning 'country of the blacks'[1] and it was originally a substantially larger land than it is today. For thousands of years their history was entwined with that of the Egyptian dynasties. This has imbued it with a rich culture and created a country of great diversity, where both Muslims and Christians, of Arab and African descent, have dissolved into a vast melting pot of different ethnic groups and languages. This was our chance to get a glimpse into this fascinating and colourful country, so having met with our agent Nazeem, and gone through the familiar port bureaucracy, we told him we wished to visit Khartoum. He was only too ready to help and assured us that he could make all the necessary arrangements.

At the same time I enlisted his help in getting our repair work done. I needed a carpenter to secure the rudders but I also wanted to find an engineer to fit an engine; by this point I had reluctantly conceded that it was the only way to deal with the realities and dangers of moving a fifty-tonne ship in and out of modern harbours. We were not able to row her and tows were proving to be extremely costly. I reconciled myself to the fact that its use would be restricted to coming in and out of ports, and the rest of the time we would be under sail. Nazeem seemed to know where we could find an engine so the following day Nick, Eric and I were taken to a large warehouse on the edge of an industrial site. It resembled a vast hangar, in which we discovered an Aladdin's Cave of mechanical equipment. Every conceivable type of old and battered engine, gearbox and lorry part was stacked inside. Most had been salvaged from accidents or dilapidated and decaying vehicles, and now they were laid out before us like museum exhibits, each encased in a thick layer of dust. A group of young men watched us intently as we peered over half-a-dozen engines before picking out the most suitable one. With no idea what we might be getting we wrote down a few details and left. From this information Alice was able to track down the engine's history and as it seemed to be what we were looking for I asked the agent to begin negotiations, while giving him the additional task of finding us an engineer to convert it to marine use.

In the meantime Nick and Rebecca departed for Khartoum and a new recruit joined the ship. Niklas Andersson was a part-time fireman and truck driver from Sweden. He was stocky and strong, a passionate sailor and keen for adventure, and he immediately fitted in with the crew. I continued my efforts to get the three Indonesians to join us. The agent was adamant that they required a special visa so I made the application and waited. I had no idea at the time this was a ploy to drag out our stay in order to extort as much money from us as possible.

Nazeem came to find me a few days later. 'Engine … for ship … eight thousand dollars,' he informed me.

'How much? No, it's not worth anything like that,' I protested.

He shrugged his shoulders. 'Eight thousand,' he repeated.

It was clear that this was not up for negotiation. They knew we needed an engine and either we accepted the price or looked elsewhere.

Nazeem continued, 'Engineer … I find for you … Mohammad. Change engine … for ship … three thousand dollars.'

Before I had time to register the first two figures he went on to tell me he had also located a carpenter.

'He do work for you … fourteen thousand dollars.'

I was convinced there was an error in this case as it should have been closer to a few hundred dollars. I went through each part of the work we needed in case there had been some misunderstanding, but there was no mistake. I was told this was the same price that any carpenter in Port Sudan would charge.

I found this hard to believe. I had expected the *hiwayan,* or foreigner's price, but this was ridiculous. Fortunately, during our forays into town, we had befriended some members of the Red Crescent, the Islamic arm of the International Red Cross, and discovered their boss knew of a carpenter in Port Sudan called Abdul Hardie. Abdul had a workshop in town so we paid him a visit. He was a big, tough-looking man and I braced myself for some hard negotiations as I explained what I wanted him to do. Abdul made a few calculations on a dirty piece of paper before declaring he would do the work for four thousand dollars. Our carpentry costs had suddenly plummeted by ten thousand dollars. Although it was still high for what we wanted I knew this was the best price we would get and I was quick to accept his offer.

Later I discovered from Abdul why our first quote had been so high. The local carpenters had effectively formed a cartel and agreed to charge an identical fee, with the one being awarded the job sharing the spoils with the rest. They could charge any amount, safe in the knowledge that no one would undercut them, but Abdul was not easily intimidated, and luckily for us he had been prepared to break ranks.

With a carpenter, an engine and an engineer, we were ready to go into dry dock. Nazeem assured me it was all in hand but after a couple of weeks of excuses I began to lose patience. When I pressed him for a date I got nowhere and then the realisation dawned that he hadn't been negotiating with the dockyard at all. A meeting with the director of the dry dock confirmed my suspicions; he knew nothing about us. Nazeem had been stringing us along, reluctant to relinquish his meal ticket. We would have to wait another week before the dock was free, but finally *Phoenicia* would get the repairs she needed.

It had been a similarly frustrating story with our travel plans. Did we need permits and visas to travel? At first nobody seemed to know. After discovering papers were required we had made the mistake of leaving it to Nazeem to arrange. Three weeks later we approached the Tourism Ministry. It transpired it was far too difficult for them to sort out but they informed us they would write to Immigration about the matter. We waited. Until visas were granted we were restricted to the port.

As the days turned into weeks Port Sudan acquired a new name – 'Port Sudon't.'

Stuck within the confines of the town, the crew took some time to relax, wander through the colourful food markets and make use of the Internet cafes to send personal messages and get news from home. John found his own distractions. He had struck up a friendship with one of the Red Crescent workers, a Norwegian woman called Anine. As our stay got longer they spent increasing amounts of time together and their friendship soon developed into something deeper.

With so much time on our hands we made what repairs we could to the ship, and exploring the local scrapyard for parts became an entertaining way to spend a few hours each day. The yard was a sprawling mass of wooden shacks, spread out as far as the eye could see. People worked and lived on site and while some hawked their goods, others repaired and rejuvenated even the most woeful pieces of equipment in their makeshift forges. Nothing was deemed too old or rusty to be saved and most mechanical parts of some description could be found.

By now we had been in Port Sudan for a month and the weather was beginning to change. As we waited to move into dry dock we experienced the first storm of the season, and it hit with a violence none of us had expected. During the evening, as the light was fading, a heaviness fell over the port and the winds started to pick up. As their force increased we removed anything on deck that could be blown away. Soon the rain began: heavy, pounding, relentless rain. As it lashed the deck we desperately tried to seal the cabin. A low, throaty rumble of thunder rolled across the port and seconds later a shard of lightning exploded from the darkness. *Phoenicia* was facing into the wind and as it gusted to gale force she suddenly lurched to starboard with a jolt; the front anchor had given way, dragging along the seabed. We had been thrown to within a few metres of a large concrete mooring buoy and dangerously close to a luxury boat anchored nearby. As the sky switched from dark to light I could see our horse's ears bobbing centimetres from the boat's window. We had to pull *Phoenicia* away before her heavy weight smashed into it. Jev and John took the inflatable to try to secure a line to a concrete buoy on our port side. Jev was controlling the outboard motor but it was dark and the wind was whipping the water up into a frenzy. Within minutes of heading out the inflatable hit a wave, tipped up and sent Jev into the angry swell. In the rush he had forgotten to put on the kill key, a safety line from wrist to ignition, and as the engine continued to rev the inflatable surged forward and shot up the side of the harbour wall, with Jev in the water and the propeller blades still turning. John had managed to hold on and cut the engine before it could slice Jev to pieces. We watched from the ship in horror but, undeterred, Jev managed to drag himself back into the inflatable and they headed for the buoy. When they discovered the rope was not going to hold *Phoenicia* they came back for an anchor and chain, then ventured into the storm again to lay it out as far from the ship as they could.

The rest of us turned our attention to repositioning the first anchor, but it was badly snagged on something and we couldn't haul it in. Eric had scrambled across to the other boat to help drag it out of the water but he hadn't noticed the broken glass on the deck. As his hand caught its jagged edge it sliced into the side of his finger and blood quickly began oozing from the cut. We cleaned and bandaged the wound, but in those conditions we knew it could easily become infected, so John left with Eric in search of a local hospital while we continued battling to get *Phoenicia* into a safe position. Our attempts to retrieve the anchor were futile. We let it go with the float attached and secured the rope to *Phoenicia*'s side. By the time we had laid out a third anchor and got the ship back into her original position it was nearly two in the morning. The storm had subsided and Eric had returned. The weather had wiped out Port Sudan's power supply, the hospital had been flooded and plunged into darkness and he had endured an uncomfortable wait before receiving a couple of injections and a painkiller. It was an experience he wished never to repeat.

Once *Phoenicia* was secure we were able to assess the damage on board. Our efforts to protect the cabin had failed and everything inside was drenched, including the computer and Jev's mobile phone. With nothing to lose, we heated the oven and left both of them inside overnight. We retired to damp bunks, every muscle aching but reassured that the ship was out of immediate danger.

The next morning we retrieved the computer; with one touch of the button it jumped back into life but Jev's phone refused to respond. Over breakfast we relived the night's events and discussed our concerns for *Phoenicia*, concluding the problem was clear: the anchor chain bought in Arwad was too light for a fifty-tonne ship and we needed to find something heavier. In the meantime we made further efforts to secure our position, fixing lines to the ships on both our port and starboard sides.

Although a similar storm blew up the following night, this time our anchors only dragged slightly.

It was a relief to be moving to dry dock, as with the rainy season underway it was not just storms with which we had to contend. Life on board was hot and uncomfortable and every night a ravenous army of mosquitoes descended on us, despite our best efforts to net our bunks. Even with all the difficulties we were facing I had no regrets starting the journey, nor any desire to be in the colder climes of the northern hemisphere. I remained convinced we would overcome any problems.

The following day we made preparations to move. By mid morning a small tug appeared to take us upriver. Ironically, having had so many problems stopping the anchors dragging, now we had great trouble hauling them up. We retrieved two but although the final anchor came up on the trip line, the chain was firmly stuck and we had no choice but to let it go. As we left it quickly became evident that the tug's captain was unaware or perhaps unconcerned of how delicately we had to travel to protect *Phoenicia*'s frame. He ignored our increasingly desperate attempts to get him to slow down as we sped upriver. Finally, just as we were about to enter the dock he cut the corner. There was a sickening grating sound as our hull made contact with the dock wall. Thankfully *Phoenicia* escaped any serious damage, although she received a lasting gash to her starboard side.

It soon became clear that the promise to haul her onto dry dock later that day would not materialise so John and Niklas decided to take the inflatable back to where we had been anchored to try to recover our chain. Niklas scrambled on board the boat that had been moored next to us to get some leverage. Despite repeated attempts to pull it up, the chain would not shift so they cut the rope and recovered the float but left the chain. They failed to notice the two men on the dockside frantically trying to get their attention.

A few minutes after they had returned to *Phoenicia* a car and motorbike came to an abrupt halt at the dock. Two men jumped out and confronted us with an angry and incomprehensible rant. It was fortunate that Nazeem happened to be on board at the time. He explained that the men were port security and were demanding to know why two of my crew had boarded the other ship.

John and Niklas returned to the scene with them to recount what they had done, but the guards refused to believe their story. Instead they accused them of stealing from the other boat and threatened to call the police. At this point the agent in charge of the other ship arrived and, having been asked to check that everything was in order, he disappeared again. John and Niklas waited nervously; if the agent backed their claims an attempt to extort money would inevitably follow. To their amazement, when he returned he thanked them for putting a line on his boat the previous night and confirmed there was nothing missing. Niklas and John returned to *Phoenicia* shortly afterwards, relieved their ordeal was over. We were tired and frustrated with the constant problems we seemed to face, and everyone wanted to get the work done and leave as soon as possible.

It had taken us a month to get *Phoenicia* to the dock, but we had to wait a further five days to be hauled out of the water and no one seemed to have an explanation for the delay. Once out we were keen to make up for lost time but coordinating the carpenters, the engineer, our agent and the dockyard was never going to be easy. This was not an ordinary ship and Port Sudan was no ordinary port. As Mohammad had not finished preparing the engine we spent the time scraping and antifouling the hull.

I was perplexed by Mohammad's lack of motivation and interest. He appeared bright, resourceful and inventive and we were paying him well. Everything had been agreed but for weeks he never turned up for work. Eventually we got to the root of the problem and it was no surprise to learn it involved our agent. It turned out that Mohammad was going to receive only a fraction of the money we were paying and the agent would pocket the rest. Had Nazeem offered him a fair price, no doubt the job would have been done much quicker; in the end it took over a month.

When Mohammad was working he was quite possibly the most resourceful person any of us had ever encountered. The dry dock doubled up as a scrapyard and if he had a problem or needed to adapt a section of the engine he would disappear in search of the correct piece. Once he had found what he was looking for he would cobble together these disparate parts, like a mad scientist absorbed with his new invention. Eventually a lump of mismatched welded metal appeared with beams, bars and pipes protruding from all directions. This was our 'marinised' engine and it demonstrated African creativity at its best.

In fact the delay with the engine didn't cost us any extra time due to another setback stemming from a misunderstanding with our carpenter, Abdul. He had turned up, as arranged, with four men and got to work removing the planks from the lower deck at the aft of the ship. Suddenly all worked stopped; they were staring down at the two tonnes of steel ballast that had to be removed before the frame for the engine could be fitted. The next thing we knew everyone had downed tools and made a quick exit. Whether he misunderstood the task we had asked of him, or when faced with the work he chose to misunderstand, was not clear. The result was the same: we had lost our workforce. We had only one option left if we wanted to get the job finished so the following day a rather disgruntled crew pushed, pulled and dragged the steel out of the bilge and off the ship. It was a sweaty, dirty and thoroughly unpleasant job, but Niklas' strength was invaluable and he seemed to relish the challenge. Once completed the carpenters returned to fit the frame.

Finally the modified truck engine could be craned up and lifted through the front hatch to the lower deck. With what would prove to be a rare example of forward planning, Mohammad produced a custom-made trolley to wheel the engine through the lower deck, past the food storage bins and into the new engine room. Everything was coming together and spirits were high. The engine was on board and we expected Mohammad to bring the shaft and propeller within the next few days so we could progress with aligning and fitting it. Unfortunately what we had interpreted as 'yes I have the shaft and propeller' actually meant 'yes I know where you can buy them, if they have them in stock'. We were losing even more precious time and our collective sense of humour had long since evaporated in the heat.

After another few days' delay and with much pushing from the crew, Mohammad located the parts. Eric calculated the angle the shaft had to exit and Abdul and his men returned to drill a hole in the sternpost. This took seven hours to complete. On first assessment it seemed a reasonable job until, on closer inspection, we discovered this hadn't been their first attempt; there were another four holes in the sternpost. I was becoming concerned that Abdul was making far too many mistakes. Other carpenters had come to the dock, threatening him for undercutting them, but this did not seem to bother him; it was more that the task was proving to be exceptionally challenging and he nearly buckled under the pressure. One evening after he had finished work he collapsed from exhaustion. I was worried about him but I also had to consider the expedition and I needed him to complete one more job, which was vital if we were ever going to get away.

Meanwhile we took the opportunity to make our own repairs and alterations. This was helped by a welcome boost of fresh energy when three Indonesian faces appeared one afternoon. I had spent two months trying to sort out special visas, but in the end they had got tired of waiting for them to materialise and Aziz had managed to obtain them in Jakarta. I was delighted to see them, and although I was still waiting to hear from Dirman, Suhra, a carpenter and sailor, had agreed to take his place for the next phase of the journey. However, Sulhan had been able to join us and I was lucky to have such an experienced crew member on board. He was a motorboat captain and had sailed thousands of miles across Indonesian waters on numerous assignments. In his late forties, he had an impish face, weathered by a life spent on the sea, and although he was small he was agile and very strong. He only knew a few words of English but I spoke some Indonesian and when that failed Aziz was on hand to translate. Within hours of arriving on board they had insisted on caulking the ship and Suhra got to work making a wooden *zuli*, a traditional Arab lavatory that hung over the portside bow and doubled up as a *mandi,* the Indonesian word for shower. Until this point we had used buckets for all ablutions and when our chemical lavatory had failed months before we had found a new use for the remaining spare buckets.

In addition Suhra and Sulhan made some adjustments to the rudders to make them stronger, but to give us more control when using the engine we added a central rudder, made by the crew from pieces of scrap metal in true Mohammad style. Eventually, after weeks of haggling, we managed to acquire some heavier anchor chain. John and Niklas had been back to the scrapyard again and again, week after week in an attempt to get a good deal. In the end we met with the owner and after four weeks of persistence we had our chain, but for barely less than the original asking price. It turned out to be worth the money as the anchors never dragged badly again. Finally, we made a new storm sail in the form of a jib, but only the crew of *Phoenicia* could have employed a partially blind man to sew it together; it was only to be expected that the measurements didn't work out at the first attempt.

By this stage the repairs and alterations had almost been completed. Now there was just one job left for the carpenters and I was determined they would deliver it on time. We needed Adbul to make and fit a block that would attach to the keel to support the protruding shaft and prop, but we were in a race against time to get finished before the Islamic holiday of Eid, when the dock would be closed for ten days. Abdul told us they would make this in their workshop and deliver it to us on the morning of 5th December. This was the day before Eid and an uncomfortably tight deadline. We had been in Sudan for a long time and I had become familiar with assurances like this, so I asked John to go to Abdul's workshop at nine the next morning to apply some gentle pressure. By eight o'clock that evening, after spending eleven hours at the workshop, the carpenters finished the job. The following morning we made a quick exit from the dockyard, just before they closed for the holiday. We were out, but over the next forty-eight hours we began to wonder if we would ever be ready to leave.

10

Our final days in Port Sudan were dominated by the discovery of a long list of unresolved issues with the ship. Some of the repairs had not been fixed as expected, whereas others didn't work at all. There were fuel leaks, incorrectly made parts and a shear pin that broke just as we were about to depart, which delayed us for another twenty-four hours. I debated whether we should stay three more days until after Christmas, but when I put it to the crew the overwhelming consensus of opinion was that we should get out as soon as possible. This was a rash decision but we had reached the limit of our patience; we bought some spare parts and prepared to leave. Sailing *Phoenicia* was going to be a struggle, but if we were going to get her fixed to the standard we required we needed to get her to Aden.

We set sail on 23rd December, greatly relieved to be on our way. We used the engine to clear the reefs and the coastline, but as we came out into open water we sailed straight into a northeast headwind. We spent the next twenty-four hours battling to make twenty miles. It had been two and a half months since we had last sailed and seasickness had taken hold of some of the crew but fortunately it soon passed. Over the following days we were so focused on getting to our next destination we hardly noticed it was Christmas.

We were making steady progress and the new rudders were working well, so as we approached the Saudi Arabian coast I decided to test the engine. What we discovered was alarming, as it wasn't long before the shear pin broke off and the engine stopped. It restarted without much trouble and fortunately we had a number of spare pins, but when we replaced it and tried again exactly the same thing happened. It was at this point we realised that the dockyard had failed to put in the keyway, which was vital for transferring power from the shaft to the propeller. We were also experiencing fuel supply problems to the engine, and both issues were beginning to cause us concern. Added to this the weather conditions were doing nothing to make life easier, and the winds and currents continued to fight our attempts to make better headway. We sailed further inland to take advantage of what we hoped would be more moderate seas, but with twenty-five knot winds we made little progress.

On New Year's Eve we anchored at the unfortunately named Pearly Gates on the Saudi-Yemeni border while we waited for the weather to improve. We decided our best option would be to try to head for Hodeidah on the Yemeni coast. Two days later, when the winds had died back and the seas calmed, we pressed on down the coast and managed to cover nearly sixty miles in twenty-four hours. This gave us a glimmer of hope and, with just over the same distance still left to sail, our prayers for calm seas and light winds to take us there were answered.

We arrived in Hodeidah on 3rd January. We ordered some critical spares and more food, and a few days later we left for Aden. It was just over two hundred miles along the coast, but if we had hoped for better sailing we were disappointed. Fighting strong southeasterly headwinds and with the current against us we were barely moving. At times a gust would even push us backwards, compounding our frustrations further. We sailed inshore as far as we dared but the winds became too strong and we were getting nowhere. We could not justify our meagre progress of less than one knot and we decided to anchor and wait for the conditions to improve. We had travelled less than a hundred miles and on the fourth day we managed only five more in twenty-four hours. I knew we had come to a critical point in the expedition. We discussed our options but everyone on board knew that the decision had been made for us already; we would have to turn around and sail back to Hodeidah. It was a bitter blow. With the winds behind us we retraced our track, and what had taken us four days to complete we managed in less than twelve hours. It was a reminder of what a sailing expedition should be like. I knew now that I would have to put the voyage on hold until April, when the winds would be more favourable again.

11

Our enforced stay in Port Sudan was having major repercussions for the expedition. We were out of step with the winds and currents that would have enabled *Phoenicia* to sail around Africa in the shortest time, and now the weather was working against us. We had been forced to admit defeat; *Phoenicia* could only sail downwind and trying to force her to sail any other way was pointless. There would be no prospect of making further progress until early spring.

Having returned to Hodeidah, we had to seek a berth in a commercial harbour. We were allocated an agent, Mohammad, who had the unhappy task of looking after the occasional yacht that was forced to come in when some difficulty or mishap had befallen it. It was no surprise that my first request to Mohammad was met with incredulity.

'We need to stay here three months until the winds change,' I explained.

He stared at me, unsure if he had heard correctly, and the request seemed to trigger a nervous twitch. He began to blink rapidly. *Phoenicia*'s arrival was going to cause him more problems than he had anticipated.

'No,' he replied, 'This ship … no … not allow.'

This was solely a commercial port and its unsuitability for other vessels was soon evident. In the days that followed we were frequently asked to move *Phoenicia* along the quay to make way for new ships unloading their goods. One morning a bulk grain carrier arrived alongside us and for a week, both day and night, loose grain poured through a pipe that stretched from the ship to a queue of waiting lorries. We were enveloped in a thick, choking cloud of grain dust and it was a miracle none of the crew developed breathing problems. We repeatedly asked to be moved but each time we received the same reply, 'Not possible.'

I knew the only chance I had to secure a berth for three months was to see the man in charge. Thirty years of dictatorship in Yemen had left many lower down the ladder of power seemingly incapable of decision making, terrified of the repercussions if anything went wrong. I made a request to see the Port Captain, in the hope that he could come up with a solution. By now I had befriended one of the tugboat engineers who had gone to college with him in India. After college the Port Captain had trained in Russia before climbing the ranks of the Yemeni Port Authority. He was considered a reasonable man and I hoped I could persuade him to let *Phoenicia* stay in the harbour until spring.

While I waited for my meeting to be arranged we made the repairs we needed to the engine. Cutting a keyway in the shaft fixed the propeller problem and it was done while still in the water, despite Eric's concerns we would flood the boat when we took the shaft and propeller out. The Indonesians had no such worries and the entire operation was completed in an afternoon.

A few days later I went to meet the Port Captain. His office was on the fourth floor of the Port Authority building overlooking the harbour. He greeted me with a smile, shook my hand and asked me to take a seat. His English was good and there were inflections of Russian underlying his strong Arabic accent. A woman, swathed in black from head to toe, brought in a tray of glasses. As she served us tea I explained to him what the Phoenicia Expedition was about, how we had come to be in Hodeidah and our need to berth the ship while we waited for the northerly winds to return to the Red Sea. He listened intently to what I had to say before making polite enquiries about my awareness of Somali pirates and the dangers of sailing around the Cape of Good Hope. I realised he was trying to work out what had possessed this eccentric Englishman to embark on such a dangerous adventure around Africa.

He explained his position, 'I cannot allow you to stay in the commercial port, we are too busy there and our space is limited. Of course the military part of the port is forbidden for security reasons. I'm not sure what else I can suggest.'

Hope was fading. The only options left were a small fishing port and another harbour a few miles away, but both would have compromised *Phoenicia*'s safety and security.

The meeting drew to a close and I rose to leave, but as he accompanied me to the door and began to wish me luck he broke off in mid-sentence and walked over to the harbour chart hanging on the wall.

'There is one possibility,' he mused as he placed his finger on the chart. 'This jetty belongs to the Maritime Affairs Authority, you could try them.'

The MAA were responsible for the maritime preservation of Yemen's coastline and the Port Captain was pointing to some moorings they used for pollution-monitoring vessels. The Director General was based in Sana'a, Yemen's capital, but he suggested we see the local man in charge, Captain Bassam.

'It's your only hope,' he added as we left his office.

In the meantime the crew had some decisions to make. There was no point in any of us staying with *Phoenicia* until April; three months living on board with little chance of being able to travel beyond the town was not an inviting prospect. Aziz, Suhra and Sulhan decided to return to Indonesia but not until the ship's berthing arrangements had been sorted out. They agreed to rejoin the expedition once *Phoenicia* had reached Aden later in the summer.

Within a couple of days Niklas had booked a ticket to Stockholm and had asked Mohammad to help him get an exit visa. Bureaucracy was typically slow, complicated further by Niklas' desire to spend some time in Sana'a before leaving. Several Western tourists had been kidnapped over the previous years and the authorities would have preferred us to go straight to the airport. He managed to talk his way out of an expensive armed escort but not the sixty-dollar charge to take out the souvenirs he had bought, which included a Yemeni sword and a *jambier,* a tribesman's traditional dagger. On the morning of his departure he was presented with another bill of fifteen dollars for port, immigration and police services. Not wishing to be delayed any longer, he paid the money and left for Sana'a.

Jev felt he needed to return home to Latvia to find more work and the time delays meant that neither Eric nor John would be able to complete the entire expedition. As both had allocated a year to the project they opted to use some of that time to travel around East Africa before returning home. John was keen to return to Sudan to see Anine. He spent several fruitless days trying to get a visa from the embassy in Sana'a but, having been foiled by the bureaucracy of the Sudanese immigration system, he decided to explore other parts of the East African coast instead.

However, leaving didn't go smoothly for Eric, John or Jev, and as the days passed tensions began to arise with Mohammad over their exit visas. Although there were wrangles over proof-of-ticket confirmation, the main problem was the charge of fifteen dollars to process their visas. Eric and Jev considered this to be a bribe and a standoff ensued. Mohammad held out for the money while they became increasingly irritated as nothing happened. Eric threatened to camp outside the immigration office while Jev bitterly complained that I hadn't replaced Mohammad with another agent. There was no reason to believe that someone else would have handled the situation differently, and I was reluctant to cause problems when I was trying to do all I could to get a berth for *Phoenicia*. Matters came to a head one afternoon when I was in the town. Eric, Jev and John took off across the dockyard to tell anyone who would listen that, as Mohammad was not doing his job, he was effectively preventing them from leaving. This soon reached the ears of the Port Authority and on my return Mohammad and I were summoned to the Police Chief's office. When I arrived I found several officers sprawled over sofas, chewing *khat*, the leaves of the local drug, seemingly oblivious to what was going on. In contrast the Police Chief was both aware and irritated by what had been happening and made it clear he was unimpressed with the behaviour of my crew. After I had been given a dressing-down I assured him there would be no further protests.

It was an assurance I could not guarantee. I knew Eric and Jev were still in no mood to compromise and I had to do something to resolve the situation quickly so I paid Mohammad the money and the following day he produced the visas. Eric, Jev and John left for Sana'a believing they had won their battle, but that evening I got a call from Mohammad. He had been detained by the police and was being held in a cell overnight.

'Help me,' he pleaded. 'This must be mistake. Why have police put me here?'

I felt for him but there was little I could do. Fortunately, the following day his ordeal came to an end when he was released without explanation or charge.

I remained in Hodeidah for a month trying to persuade the MAA to give *Phoenicia* a berth. The final decision rested with the Director General in Sana'a, but with the help and support of Captain Bassam and his colleagues *Phoenicia* was given permission to stay on their jetty until April. After this I would sail her south to Aden, where I would remain until the winds would allow us to get to Oman.

I left Yemen and returned to London. The setback to the timing of the expedition was a big disappointment and it would be another six months before we could get back on track. It was a shame that some of the crew could no longer complete the journey, but I knew I would find more people to take part. What was of greater concern to me was how some of our supporters would react. I did not want them to think that I had abandoned the expedition and would allow the project to fade away, as *Phoenicia* languished in a Yemeni port. I knew how important it was to keep enthusiasm for the expedition alive. It would take longer than planned but I was determined the voyage would continue.

II

I returned to Hodeidah during the first week of May for the start of the next phase of the expedition. John was the only member of the previous crew to return, accompanied by Nigel Fransham and Richard Kellie, two supporters of the project who had stepped in to help me out.

Seeing *Phoenicia* again was a little like getting re-acquainted with an old friend, familiar and reassuring but with the sense something subtle had changed. In *Phoenicia*'s case the mast now had a crow's nest of the feathered variety rather than the nautical one, but apart from that she was in good shape. It was still tough work getting her ready to sail again after three months, and days of hard work had left the crew covered in rope burns, cuts and bruises; every bone and muscle ached but our efforts were coming together. We managed to fix a couple of leaks, but although MAA engineers worked on the generator for hours they could not bring it back to life. Our power would have to come from the solar panels, wind generator and engine alternator. This would give us the bare essentials of communication and lights at night, which was just enough to keep us going if we were careful how we used it.

We put the word around town that we needed crew and within days we had recruited three Yemeni sailors, bringing our numbers up to seven. This gave us enough manpower for the next leg, but despite being ready to leave the wind had not complied with our plans and continued to blow from the south. The locals assured us it would turn in a few days so we waited. Just under a week later, as predicted, the wind switched direction and we set sail for Aden, two hundred and seventy miles south along the Yemeni coast. We negotiated our way back down the long and difficult ten-mile channel and by mid afternoon we had reached the open sea. We began well, with a westerly wind blowing on our quarter, but May is a transition time for the winds in the Red

Sea, when they turn from mainly southerlies to northerlies. In the process I knew the wind direction would be erratic, changing regularly or even disappearing completely.

The crew settled in well and began to get to grips with the routine on board. We were divided into two watches: Nigel led one with John and two Yemeni hands, Ali and Fadh, while I took the second with Richard and the other Yemeni sailor, Abdul. Unfortunately Richard was a little seasick and Abdul didn't like to overexert himself so the bulk of the work was down to me. Nevertheless Richard was an entertaining watch companion for someone interested in history. A writer and historian, he had spent fifteen years working on a book about the Holy Land, which he still hadn't finished. It was reassuring to know I wasn't the only one with a dogged determination that went beyond the bounds of normal reason.

On the third day at sea we began our approach to Bab el-Mandeb. Here the Red Sea funnels into a narrow strait between Yemen and Djibouti before passing into the Gulf of Aden. In Arabic it means 'Gate of Tears', a name that has taken on a new significance with the threat now posed by piracy. Every week vast amounts of traffic, travelling between the Mediterranean and the Indian Ocean, pass through this point. This includes tankers transporting millions of barrels of oil, which has made it an extremely attractive place for a would-be hijacker.

With this in mind I had spent considerable time on anti-piracy measures. I had run through a security briefing two days before we left and we knew the drill. It would have been possible for us to buy AK47s for ten dollars each in Hodeidah but we had resisted the temptation. As much as we would have liked to wrap the ship's rails with barbed wire and razor blades and have Molotov cocktails at the ready, in reality there was very little we could do to stop pirates coming on board. Our plan was to stay a few miles from the Yemeni shoreline, darken the ship at night and observe radio silence. We hoped our sonic device, the LRAD, would help delay any assault on the ship while we alerted the authorities by satellite phone. We were in frequent contact with the local coalition forces patrolling the seas and Drum Cussac, our security advisers, kept us updated regularly with news of the latest attacks. Although I knew merchant ships were the main targets for pirates, smaller vessels were easier prey and many had been taken. In these cases the crew, not their cargo, held the greatest ransom value and hostages faced imprisonment, torture and even death.

Given this, when a small wooden boat started making its way towards us as we approached the strait, I began to feel tense. As they got closer the men stood up and before I knew what was happening my Yemeni crew began waving and calling to them.

'What are you doing?' I shouted, suddenly panicking that they were inviting pirates to take the ship.

Abdul, Ali and Fadh looked confused then smiled and pointed to the men, who by now were holding up a catch of fish. What I had feared was an attempted kidnap was, in reality, an act of kindness. They threw some of the fish on board so we could share the spoils of a hard day's work and that evening, instead of spending the night under armed guard, we enjoyed a traditionally cooked Yemeni meal of fish, rice, tomatoes and strong red chillies.

It was a relief but I knew we were still not out of danger. By the time we entered the strait it was dark and an hour of nerve-wracking sailing lay ahead. To make the journey even more precarious an island, housing a local military base, divides the strait in two and we were restricted to a narrow channel one mile wide and three miles long. Although strong winds were pushing us through this small stretch of water the tide was against us and at times we slowed to just over a knot. We focused on negotiating the currents and avoiding other ships, but progress felt agonisingly slow. We were close enough to shore to see the car headlights as traffic moved along the coastal road and it felt as if we would end up on the shore if we made one wrong move, but we had been warned not to drift too close to the military exclusion zone. This was because they had been known to approach those who strayed into, or even near, this area to demand money.

After we had got out into the main channel our progress began to improve and the winds grew stronger until we had reached a speed of four knots. Despite expecting a change in wind direction once we reached the Gulf of Aden the fresh westerlies remained for another twenty miles. We took advantage of this while we could, even though at times steering was difficult. As we travelled between the coasts of Yemen and Somalia we remained in dangerous waters for piracy, and to avoid detection we observed radio silence and continued to sail without navigation lights at night. To our alarm we discovered that some container ships did the same. Fortunately, as we spent the week of our journey hugging the coast, we saw little traffic but it was crucial to keep a good lookout.

We reached Aden a week later where we moored in the main harbour, next to the military port. There was no need to search for the agent, he found us. Omar kept a watch on all vessels coming in and going out of the harbour. He was a local taxi driver but earned extra money by looking after boats and helping with visas and customs.

With a refreshingly honest approach he told me how things worked. 'You pay money … done quicker … you don't want … that is okay too.'

I felt I could trust him and he agreed to look after *Phoenicia* for the next three months until we were due to sail to Oman, keeping an eye on her and pumping her bilges every few days. He told me that two anchors would be enough to secure her but I insisted on three, two at the bow and one at the stern. He thought this was unnecessary but agreed this was how she would stay.

III

I went back to England to make preparations for phase two of the expedition and returned to Aden again in August. Omar informed me that there had been such big storms during my absence that two boats had lost their moorings and had taken off across the harbour. I was relieved to discover that *Phoenicia*, with three anchors holding her, had not been one of them. The crew began to appear shortly after I arrived. Sulhan and Aziz were the first to return but this time they were accompanied by Dirman. I was delighted he had finally been able to join us, as his skills and attitude would bring much to the expedition. He was in his mid thirties and a ship's carpenter, although he seemed to have a magic touch when it came to fixing mechanical equipment too. He was quiet and modest and greeted everyone with a broad smile, revealing a gleaming set of large white teeth. He had an incredible ability to remain cheerful at all times regardless of what was going on around him because, for Dirman, life was an endlessly positive and happy experience.

Over the following week crew arrived from all over the world until we were up to seven. Warren Aston flew in from Australia and Doug Smith from the UK, while Paul Reid, an American, made the relatively short journey from Sana'a where he had been working as a graphic designer. *Phoenicia* had been generating a fair amount of interest during her time in Aden and while I was waiting for the full contingency of crew to arrive, two hundred Yemeni high school students came to learn about Phoenician history and have a tour of the ship. One morning a Yemeni navy officer arrived with a slightly more unusual request: he asked if I would be prepared to let *Phoenicia* be used in a piracy exercise. They wanted to show a Russian TV station their anti-piracy measures and *Phoenicia*'s resemblance to a pirate boat made her perfect for the part. They explained that they would come on board and stage a mock pirate arrest, and as it seemed to be harmless enough I agreed. The Russian TV crew set up their cameras on deck ready for action. A huge patrol boat, at least twice *Phoenicia*'s size, came up beside us and as her skipper reversed alongside, the boat swung round and its stern caught our hull. It had been nothing more than a slight touch but it was followed by a loud crack. As men scrambled on board brandishing guns I desperately tried to see what had happened. In ten minutes the entire exercise was over. The apologies were profuse but the damage was done: the patrol boat had split one of *Phoenicia*'s planks. Fortunately it was just above the waterline and Dirman managed to nail a small piece of wood against the crack and seal it with resin.

Just over a week later we went into dry dock, as *Phoenicia* still needed a general overhaul before we sailed again. I had negotiated a reasonable price at the dockyard by ensuring we did much of the work ourselves. This meant we had to spend several days in temperatures of forty degrees scraping off the vast amounts of barnacles and coral clinging to the hull. However, on seeing the work involved Paul promptly disappeared again, telling me he needed to visit some friends but promising to be back by the time we left.

Once cleaned, we could see the hull was in good shape and only needed minor repairs and adjustments, but despite several attempts to fix the generator it refused to work. Finally we put on a coat of anti-fouling paint and we were ready to leave. The morning we were due to come out of dry dock I went to see the deputy at the dockyard to settle my account, only to find when he produced the bill the price had doubled. We argued for an hour over the new charges, but he refused to back down and I was becoming exasperated. In the end he fixed me with a defiant look.

'Water gone down. Ship in water today not possible. Come back tomorrow,' he told me.

He was right, the dispute had cost us our chance to get away that day, but I was not going to pay the extra money. I wanted to see his boss, but Omar had a better idea and suggested that a personal payment to the deputy would probably resolve the situation in the quickest possible time. As I was not prepared to wait the deputy received a small sum and the cost of the work dropped to just over the original bill. We would go back in the water at the next high tide, six o'clock the following morning.

I gave the crew a briefing on what would happen the next day.

As I was finishing, Paul, who had recently returned, interjected, 'It'll never happen. They don't work at six in the morning. You'll find they won't turn up.'

I was taken aback by his comments. Paul was new to the expedition, this was my first briefing and he was disagreeing with me already. Omar was present so I turned to him for confirmation.

'Yes, yes' he nodded, 'they come.'

By this point everyone was exhausted so we took the opportunity to get a good night's sleep. At six the following morning the dock workers appeared as promised, and we moved off the slipway and back into the water.

Plans followed to check and test the ship's equipment and we rehearsed the drill with the LRAD, our sonic deterrent. With our earplugs fitted I gave several blasts to make sure it worked and then it was covered; I hoped it would never be needed. The winds looked promising and we prayed the southwest monsoon would keep any pirates at bay for a few more days.

We were back at sea again and on our way to Salalah, the most southerly port in Oman. With a small crew of seven we had to work hard, and there was little spare time to rest but conditions were good. For security reasons we kept our contact with the outside world to a minimum. We saw very few vessels, only a couple of container ships and a handful of small boats, but to avoid attracting unwanted attention we continued to sail without navigation lights at night. Although this was not the best sailing practice, security was paramount and one evening, with the full moon illuminating our way, we were able to touch speeds of nearly five knots. Our progress remained steady until halfway through the journey, when the winds dropped and *Phoenicia* began to slow.

It was early the next morning, shortly after my watch had taken over, when Dirman suddenly shouted from the helm, 'Boss, look there.'

As I followed the direction of his arm I could see a flash of white fifteen metres from the beam of the ship.

'What the hell was that?' I asked.

He shook his head. We looked again but it had disappeared. I shouted for all hands on deck, knowing a pirate boat could be lurking in the blackness. The sleeping crew woke, immediately alert as the adrenalin began to flow, and there was a rush of activity as we prepared the LRAD and satellite phone connections. Doug got the searchlight ready then we waited and watched. The minutes ticked by, each one feeling longer than the last, but there was no movement beyond the ship except the rhythmic lapping of the waves. We continued to wait as all eyes scanned the water.

After ten minutes Dirman broke the silence, 'Big fish boss.'

'Really, Dirman?'

He shrugged his shoulders.

Doug let out a long sigh, 'You really had me going there.'

The tension began to lift. Perhaps Dirman had been right, it had been a large white shark coming up for air, or maybe the foam on the crest of a wave had played tricks on an exhausted crew. We would never know but we were in dangerous waters and we had to be alert at all times.

As the journey progressed we realised we had a problem with the engine and our batteries were no longer fully charged. In addition, as all our efforts to get the generator to work had failed, we continued to rely on our solar panels and wind generator for power. This only gave us enough for our navigation instruments, and as we were unable to use the fridge we had opted for a cool box instead. Unfortunately this had meant that most of the fresh produce and our entire store of bread had turned mouldy rapidly in the heat. I put Dirman in charge of catching fish and when we spotted a school of ten large dorado swimming around the ship he fashioned an ingenious lure made from coloured cracker packaging. Although it swam beautifully the big catch escaped him. Undeterred, he continued his efforts until he had hooked a fish, just in time for supper. Paul decided everyone needed a British meal of fish and chips and disappeared to prepare the food. Some time later we rushed to help when panicked shouts of 'Fire, fire' rose from the galley. While removing the chips from the rocking oven the tray had tipped forward and the oil had caught alight. Luckily by the time we reached him the flames had been doused and *Phoenicia* saved from serious damage.

By the end of the first week the conditions changed and the seas became very rough, with the swell reaching four metres. Normally this type of sea would be accompanied by strong winds but the lack of any breeze had cut our speed in half, and instead of making progress all the waves seemed to do was to rock the boat violently. We experienced the same phenomenon a few days later, in fact the wind stubbornly refused to return for days. At first light, after one particularly frustrating period of directionless bobbing, Aziz threw an empty noodle box over the portside to see what would happen. Thirty minutes later it appeared on our starboard side; we had been going round in circles all night. It was tedious for everyone but there was little we could do. It wasn't until the morning of the tenth day that the wind changed both direction and speed and we began to head east at two knots. As we crossed the border between Yemen and Oman we had only sixty miles left to sail. By this time we had eaten our way through most of the fresh food on board and had to resort to our plentiful stores of packets and tins. Imaginative cooking was required to disguise the corned beef and lentils that started to come out of the hold.

As we got closer to our destination Paul began ruminating on the thorny issue of how we would get into harbour. As the battery had run down we would not be able to use the engine to negotiate our way in, and this had been worrying him. Paul's entire body of sailing experience had taken place on a lake in the States; he had never sailed offshore before and our voyage had not been an entirely comfortable experience for him. We were ten miles off the coast when he suggested that we anchor until we sorted out the problem.

'The water is over a mile deep here. It's impossible to anchor,' I explained.

He thought about it for a while before coming up with another suggestion.

'Two of us should use the dinghy to go ashore,' he announced.

'We don't have enough petrol to get ten miles in the dinghy and when you run out a search party will be needed to rescue you. It's far safer to stay on board. We'll be fine,' I assured him.

I doubted whether he was convinced but he had run out of suggestions and said no more on the subject.

On 12th September we sighted the coastline of Salalah. The sun was setting and the crew stood on deck as we sailed past an impressive line of container ships unloading their goods. It was dark by the time we reached the sheltered marina. Members of Oman Sail, an Omani maritime heritage project, had been alerted to our arrival and a small group came out by boat to meet us. They gave us two new batteries to start the engine for the berthing process, much to Paul's relief.

We had arrived, just over twelve days after leaving Aden. It was coming up to Ramadan but my Indonesian crew were not allowed off the boat without a visa and they were unable to go to the mosque. It took days to get them passes so they could go ashore but once this had been done I flew back to England for a short time. *Phoenicia* would have to remain in Salalah for just over a month while we waited for the monsoon winds to blow.

The first planks are added to the keel

Dowels used to lock the mortise and tenon joints

The framing for the bunks is added to the completed hull

The hull comes together

Local children play with their new toy

Early sea trials

The departure ceremony

The First Lady of Syria with boatbuilder Khalid Hammoud and (right) talking to the crew

Getting a tow to Port Berenice

Rudder strengthening

John scales the mast

The Captain's birthday

The fruit and vegetable market Port Sudan

Abdul Hardie at work

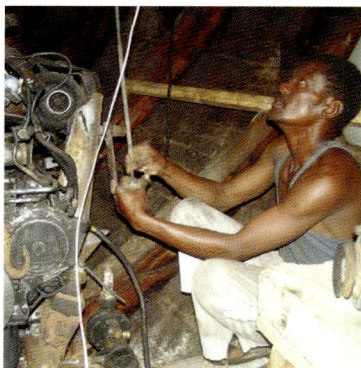

Mohammad with our engine Port Sudan

John and Niklas grab some sleep

A passing container ship

Mayotte's turtle beach

Supper at sea – clockwise from left, Sulhan, Niklas, Steph, Alice, Nick, Yuri and Keith

Phoenicia moored in the muddy tidal waters of Beira

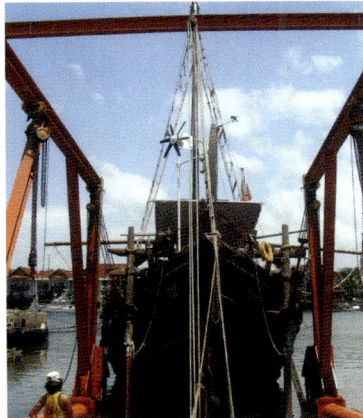
Repairs – Richards Bay

Cape Town

Celebrations in Cape Town – from left,
Steph, Vera, Yuri, Clinton, Daniel, Phllip,
Alice, Dirman and Len

Pulling up the yard

James Bay, St Helena

Ascension

Daniel, Peter, Clinton and Steph celebrate with King Neptune after crossing the Equator

Peter swims with the whale shark

Sulhan gutting fish

Philip and Dirman play chess

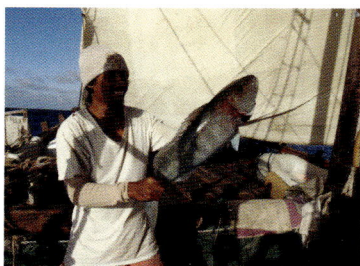
Dirman proudly shows off his catch

Keeping fit

Not the best time to go to the heads!

Sailing in the north Atlantic

Rough seas

Edward on the quay in Horta, Azores

Sulhan at the helm

The Rock of Gibraltar

Malta

Sidon

Phoenicia is covered in Lebanese flags on her arrival in Tripoli

Boats gather to meet us as we approach Arwad

Clinton's arrival celebration

Dancers on the quay

The crowds welcome us back

'I strongly advise you not to do this.'

I turned over the words in my head. It was mid October and despite this warning I was returning to Salalah so that I could take advantage of the northeast monsoon winds that would help us reach Tanzania. I had been suffering from abdominal pain and during the weeks I had been in England investigations had revealed an inflamed gall bladder. It needed to be removed and the specialist had been clear about the risks if I didn't have it done.

'If this flares up again it could burst and if you're out at sea with no medical help you will die,' he informed me.

This left me with a problem: it was a week before I was due back in Oman and I had a crew of eight about to fly out to meet me there. I didn't want to let them down and I knew if I missed this weather window the expedition would be over for another year, but I was potentially risking my life by carrying on with the journey. I spent an evening with a friend and medic pondering my dilemma. The next stage of the voyage was more than two and a half thousand miles and I anticipated it would take four to five weeks. After much deliberation we concluded that the probability of it becoming a medical emergency during this time was relatively low. I decided to take my chances and hope for the best.

As soon as I set foot in Salalah I focused my thoughts on getting the ship ready, and any other worries were pushed firmly away. Aziz, Sulhan and Dirman had arrived, Niklas had returned from Sweden and Yuri Sanada, a filmmaker, had flown in from Brazil with camera equipment in tow to record the journey. With Nick Swallow's help we had managed to recruit four sailors from the Royal Navy of Oman, except with the delays the original line up had all but been replaced. It appeared the new recruits – Khalifa, Ali, Youssof and Rashid – had little idea what they had let themselves in for and some of them seemed quite bewildered when they saw *Phoenicia*.

'Where's the satellite TV?' Youssof and Khalifa wanted to know as they came on board.

They were going to be in for a shock.

Although the crew had assembled there was a considerable amount to sort out before we left. After we had rigged the mainsail and secured the ship for sea, which took half a day, we picked up a new generator and went through a thorough victualling exercise for what would be our longest leg so far. Among the items we lugged on board were three tonnes of water, thirty kilos of potatoes and rice, ten kilos of onions, twenty kilos of pasta, two hundred packets of Indonesian noodles and enough apples and oranges to start a grocery store. A thousand tea bags would see us through many days at sea, as would ample supplies of Omani coffee; we soon realised one cup would keep us awake and wired not only for our watch but also for much of the following one.

I went through a pirate briefing with the crew. While I wanted everyone to have a positive attitude to our journey they needed to be aware of the dangers we faced. The recent attacks in the region meant we would have to alter our course to give the pirates as wide a berth as possible. When I had first planned the expedition the advice had been to stay east of fifty-eight degrees, but gradually this had increased to sixty then sixty-two, and by the time we left Oman we had been warned to keep east of sixty-five degrees. Of course the real advice was not to embark on the journey unless absolutely necessary. For me it was, so instead of following the coastline around the Horn of Africa we would head east into the Arabian Sea for more than seven hundred miles, as far away from the pirates as we could get. From that position we would turn and head south.

By the evening of Sunday 25th October *Phoenicia* and her crew were ready to leave and we set sail in warm weather and calm seas. I had divided us into two groups of five, for watches four hours long during the day and six at night, to allow everyone to get a decent amount of sleep.

Initially we struggled to make progress east. We were dependent on the winds and currents to take us where we needed to go, but although the monsoon winds had begun to blow, they were light and were taking us in a more southerly direction. It took a few days until the winds strengthened and we could replace the storm sail with the mainsail. We needed the entire crew to haul it up but it was worth the effort; our speed increased to four knots and we began to enjoy some magnificent sailing. She must have been a beautiful sight from a distance with her mainsail billowing in the wind. For the first time it gave us a true taste of the exhilaration and excitement of sailing a Phoenician ship.

We were making better progress but we still needed to be a minimum safe distance of between six and nine hundred miles from shore. By this point almost daily pirate attacks were taking place and we were only four hundred miles east, too close to the Somali coast for comfort. We consoled ourselves with the knowledge that most of the recent attacks had been several hundred miles to the south and we diverted our thoughts to life on board.

The crew had quickly fallen into a routine of watches, pumping the bilges, making sail adjustments and preparing food. The majority was Muslim and every day before they laid out their rugs on the deck to pray one of them would come to me to ask the same question, 'Where is two-seven-two?' Two-seven-two degrees was the bearing they used in Oman to point them towards Mecca. I tried to explain that the same co-ordinate that pointed them west when sailing in the waters around Muscat would no longer serve their purpose once we were out in the Indian Ocean, southeast of Mecca. As much as I tried to persuade them this bearing was now wrong they adamantly refused to believe me, so every day I would point in the direction they wanted and they would disappear to pray to a small village somewhere in East Africa.

As we sailed further from land it became noticeable how much the frequency of praying increased, and as it did I realised we were facing a problem. They were using over a litre of drinking water to wash themselves before each prayer session and now this was happening five times a day. We were carrying three thousand litres and we were facing the prospect of a third of our total supply being used this way. We had a limited amount of water for all our needs and however long or short this leg would be it had to last. The rest of us tried as hard as we could to adapt to the new circumstances by using more seawater for cooking and washing, but I knew the situation couldn't continue.

While I worked out how to deal with this problem we were reminded of a potentially more serious threat to our welfare. Although we had been making good progress, by the second week we remained over a hundred miles within the high-risk piracy area and one morning we caught sight of a small Somali vessel heading northeast. Every small boat like this had the potential to be a pirate skiff and we had no way of telling if what we could see was a threat or simply a fisherman going about his trade. All we could do was watch, our eyes transfixed by this dot bobbing around on the ocean. Gradually it became smaller and smaller until it melted into the horizon and we could breathe more easily. *Phoenicia* was vulnerable and we knew it. It wasn't until the evening, as the light was beginning to fade, that Yuri spotted something on our starboard side.

~

'I can see a light'

'It's a large ship about twenty metres, the same size as *Phoenicia*.'

'It could be a fishing boat. If not it's a pirate mother ship.'

'Wow their deck lights are bright. They're either hauling in nets or launching a skiff.'

'Looks like it's getting closer.'

'Yuri, get the generator started and the LRAD plugged in. Niklas check the satellite phone is ready and switch on our navigation lights. You're twenty degrees off course. For God's sake concentrate. We could be in real trouble here.'

'They've turned off their deck lights but their navigation lights are still on. Darken ship and turn our navigation lights off. They'll know we've seen them but if they're coming for us let's not make it easy for them. They'll have trouble finding us in the dark and the moon won't rise for an hour yet.'

'Wait. There's another contact on our portside. I can see several lights.'

'What is it?'

'This one's very large, a container ship.'

'It's going to clear us easily.'

'Then concentrate on our starboard contact.'

'Oh shit it's turning … It's coming right for us.'

'Keep quiet everyone, there's nothing we can do now except sit tight and wait.'

'The light's coming closer. It's right on top of us now. It's moving down our starboard side.'

'Where the hell is it?'

'It's not slowing, it's going to go past us. It must be a fishing boat.'

'Thank God. I hope we don't see any more tonight, I don't think my nerves can take it.'

'Stand down everyone but you must stay extremely vigilant at all times unless you want an enforced holiday in a Somali cave.'

'Right. What's for supper and are there any of those pancakes left?'

For the next few days we continued sailing out into the Indian Ocean, then just as we reached the edge of the high-risk zone where we could start our journey south, the wind changed again and pushed us further east towards India. We may have been struggling to get the direction we wanted but at least the sailing was good. We had a force six wind and the sail was hoisted high into the sky with brailing lines pulled aft, just as I had seen depicted on one of the 6th century BC Greek vases at the British Museum. *Phoenicia* surfed along the rolling waves that were hitting her starboard quarter and as the wind strength increased further the waves began to reach five metres, with crisp white horse's heads forming on their crests. With our speed climbing to seven knots we were in danger of going too fast and placing excessive pressure on the mast. To slow us down we hauled on the brailing lines to reduce the size of the mainsail. It was a primitive but effective form of reefing the sails and one that the Phoenicians had invented. It kept our speed to a manageable five knots.

As we continued to head away from the African coast, a bewildered Omani crew became increasingly anxious. By now their lack of sailing experience was beginning to show. They had been used to large naval ships, luxurious in comparison to *Phoenicia* and they had never sailed outside Omani waters before. As a result the finer points of sailing without using engine power were lost on them and they found our constant need to adapt to the conditions baffling.

'We change course … why?' one of them would ask.

I tried to explain but they seemed unable to grasp that a ship under sail had to change with the wind and it was not within our power to go in whatever direction we chose. I showed them the charts so they could get a better understanding, but they were neither persuaded nor particularly interested.

With our journey time increasing I knew I would have to tackle our water consumption so I decided to talk to Aziz. It did not go well; his face fell as I explained we had to stop using our fresh water supply for washing.

'No need for this,' he told me. 'Allah will protect us … it will be okay.'

He felt I had singled out the Muslim crew unfairly, but I had to put our drinking water needs before any other use. I knew that in Islam if a Muslim was in the desert he was permitted to wash with sand, and if there was no fresh water available sea water was acceptable, so I stood my ground. It was an awkward moment but he accepted it and passed the message on to the others.

Not long after this we were forced to change our route again. On 12th November we received reports of two very recent pirate attacks on ships only a hundred miles in front of us. One of the ships had escaped but the other had not been so lucky. It was a Greek-owned carrier called *Filitsa* and it had been on its way to Durban when it was hijacked a thousand miles east of Mogadishu. The chase had lasted five hours before the vessel and her twenty-two crew, three Greeks and nineteen Filipinos, were forced to turn around and head towards Somalia. This was alarming for two reasons: the attacks were outside the official danger zone and they had taken place in an area directly on *Phoenicia*'s intended course. With every indication that a pirate mother ship was in the area we took action immediately and diverted east towards the Maldives. Fortunately strong winds allowed us to cover two hundred and eighty miles in forty-eight hours, taking us a comfortable distance from the area of the attacks. In the next few days three ships were hijacked. Had we not diverted our course we would have sailed straight into the path of the pirates.

It had not escaped our attention that while we were making every effort to avoid putting ourselves in danger it must have appeared to other vessels that we were the problem. A reconstruction of a two and a half thousand-year-old Phoenician ship probably looked uncannily like a pirate boat to other seafarers, and on more than one occasion it seemed as if cargo ships changed direction when they saw us.

We continued to watch for any dots on the horizon as we turned our thoughts to running repairs. Four of the brailing lines, which enabled the main sail to be furled, had broken and needed to be renewed. They were made of hemp and had succumbed to the tough conditions. It was a stark reminder of how much weight hung over our heads and it must have been a risk the Phoenicians treated very seriously. When the parell, the rope that brings the mast and yard together, had snapped a week earlier it had left the yard flapping loose, away from the mast. For our safety we had changed it to a modern, thick fibre rope and Dirman had ventured aloft with the help of the bosun's chair to put an additional parell in place, just in case our replacement failed.

On 14th November we left the northern hemisphere behind as we crossed the Equator. For those who had never crossed this line under sail before we celebrated in time-honoured tradition, by arranging a reception with King Neptune. With no alcohol on board it was a modest celebration but it was an important step on our journey. It also meant we were heading for what I knew could be the most testing part of this leg.

A few days later we entered the ITCZ or Inter Tropical Conversion Zone. Located just below the Equator, it is where the weather systems of north and south meet. At this point the winds begin to lose their power and become much more unpredictable. We were three degrees south and I expected to find the southeast trade winds, which would help propel us quickly towards East Africa, somewhere between six and eight degrees. Unfortunately nature had other plans and over a week later we were more than eight degrees south, still in the clutches of the ITCZ, and with little sign of any trade winds. One day we travelled just thirteen miles, but this was an improvement on the twenty-four hours we spent drifting around in circles. Hopes were raised a few miles short of nine degrees when the wind started to pick up. We hoisted the mainsail in excited anticipation, but a few hours later it vanished as quickly as it had arrived and we were becalmed again, with only the current to carry us forward. We entered our fourth week at sea with no clear view as to when we would reach landfall, and it was beginning to test everyone's patience. These were the frustrations of sailing a Phoenician ship and familiar to every sailor before the advent of the engine.

As we continued to drift, the Omanis began to doubt the trade winds actually existed. I knew sailing vessels had used them for hundreds, arguably thousands, of years but it was hard to be convincing when the evidence appeared to the contrary. As we floated around in the ITCZ they began to get agitated.

'Our families ... they worry ... not know where we are,' Ali complained.

This wasn't strictly true as we were sending daily blogs to the *Phoenicia* website and, in addition to this, the satellite tracker on board regularly updated our position. We knew a naval officer in Oman was picking these up and keeping the families informed, but to help morale I arranged for them to call home on the satellite phone. Each one had only two minutes to talk to their families but it had the desired effect and for a short time their protests and complaints ceased.

However, the ITCZ had another downside: coupled with our slow progress we were now beset by tropical storms. Downpours followed in quick succession and lightning continually lit up the horizon. With each deluge our clothes and bunks became saturated and they barely had time to dry before the next storm hit. Even though this gave us the opportunity for a freshwater shower, and allowed Aziz to top up our drinking water supplies, it was having a negative impact on the crew.

To make matters worse our fresh fish supplies had almost entirely vanished. Up to this point fishing had been so good we had a competition in progress. Dirman and Sulhan, both skilled fishermen, had taken up the challenge with relish, and with the added incentive of money to be earned for catching dinner competition was fierce. For weeks we landed tuna, dorado and squid; even a shark took the bait, although as we were dragging it on board the hook snapped and it broke away. On some nights we didn't need to put out a line as suicidal flying fish would throw themselves on deck. Now days would go by without a single catch and Dirman's cheerful refrain that the fish were 'sleeping' was wearing a little thin.

One evening, after a particularly heavy downpour, Sulhan disappeared into the galley to prepare supper. Spirits began to lift as the rich warming aroma of spices cut through the salty dampness in the air. Rumour went around the ship that he was preparing noodles with flying fish, which we assumed he had found on deck. Everyone was looking forward to our first decent meal in days. We eagerly tucked in but after a few hastily swallowed mouthfuls our enthusiasm began to wane and one by one the chewing stopped. The spices could not mask an overpowering taste of fish. A few concerned glances were exchanged until eventually I plucked up the courage to ask what everyone was wondering.

'Sulhan where's the fish from?'

As I pointed at the dish he gave me a cheeky grin and produced a small packet. Everyone recognised it immediately. He had caught a few fish in Salalah and, after drying them on the roof of the cabin, had stored them in a crisp bag. That crumpled bag was now lying on the table, devoid of its contents. We had cleared the cabin roof a couple of weeks before and every one of us regretted not throwing the fish away when we had got the chance. To save us from any more improvised dishes, when fish was scarce we began to consume the stores of canned food we had brought with us.

Unfortunately this didn't prevent food becoming the focus for many of the frustrations and niggles that began to surface as the weeks at sea continued. We had started out enjoying a varied diet and a new surprise every time a different nationality was cooking. However, there were vastly differing tastes on board. The Indonesians loved spices, and the more flavour and heat they could add to a dish the better. Yuri detested spicy food, in fact he disliked any additional seasoning and could often be found trying to persuade Aziz to tone down his cooking. The Omanis seemed happy with our diet until the supplies of fresh produce gradually dwindled, and as we finished the last of many items tensions began to increase. Often they could be heard complaining, 'There's no chicken, no food.' There may have been no chicken but we weren't short of supplies, the problem was they didn't like everything we had to offer. We had plenty of canned and dried provisions to keep us going but they refused to eat tinned food past its sell-by date, unless it was something they liked, then they would waive this rule and tuck in without a murmur. When it came to breakfast, their taste for spaghetti and raisins laden with large amounts of sugar was unpalatable to the rest of us, and we were relieved when we ran out of sugar in the fifth week. Crucially, water supplies were holding up as Aziz had been able to collect enough rainwater to augment our stocks, so while the last days of the leg were not as comfortable as some would have liked, I knew we would neither starve nor go thirsty.

Finally, at nine degrees south, thirty-three days after leaving Salalah we picked up the southeast trade winds. During the early part of the morning the light winds became gusts and five-metre waves began slapping against our port quarter. Our speed had increased to over four knots and *Phoenicia* was taking most of the waves in her stride. Occasionally one would hit forward of the beam and there would be an almighty shudder as the timbers took a hard pounding. We braced ourselves each time the ship rolled and the sail flapped wildly, but composure was quickly restored before we surfed down another large wave. I began to wonder how much punishment a wooden ship that was pegged together could take. For three days we averaged just under a hundred miles a day as we continued to head southwest towards even better and more consistent winds.

It was during this time that we received word of two new piracy attacks to the west and southwest of our position. This put them between the Seychelles and Dar es Salaam, our intended destination. Having come rather too close for comfort to a group of pirates to the northeast of the Seychelles, we took the decision to divert to Mayotte, one of the Comoros islands. This left us with another nine hundred miles to go and, assuming the trade winds continued to blow, I estimated we would be there by the second week of December. Although our security advisers pointed out that pirates were operating quite close to the Comoros, at least by diverting to Mayotte we were reducing our chances of being hijacked. This caused further agitation with the Omanis.

'Why not go to Tanzania?' Khalifa asked.

The navy had promised them a two-week holiday in Zanzibar as a reward for their efforts, but now we were travelling to a different destination and the journey was taking much longer than expected. I explained our change of course but they appeared to have no perception of the threat.

'No problem. We are safe … we are Omani navy,' they assured me.

It was pointless trying to explain that all of us were valuable as hostages, regardless of our nationality; I knew pirates were still holding three Yemeni fishermen who had been hijacked a few months earlier and their captors were demanding fifty barrels of oil in exchange for them and their boat.

As our journey continued it appeared their faith in the friendly relations Oman had with other countries was boundless.

'Why we cannot stop here?' Rashid wanted to know, as he pointed at the map.

The island his finger had obliterated was Diego Garcia.

I tried to contain my exasperation, 'Because it's a US military base … high security … not allowed … and two hundred miles out of our way,' I told him.

He insisted that as Oman was on good terms with America it would be fine. I knew the US navy there had a reputation for being particularly unhelpful to yachtsmen except in cases of dire emergency. I wondered how welcoming they would be when we appeared in our little wooden boat, looking unnervingly like pirates, with an unhealthy craving for chicken.

Unsurprisingly as we came closer to other islands on our way to Mayotte the calls for us to divert got louder.

'We go to Seychelles. Stop there ... get food,' Youssof insisted.

Aziz wasn't helping the situation either. 'Philip you can change course, it will make them happy.'

Making them happy wasn't my immediate priority and the last thing I needed was another member of my crew raising their unrealistic expectations. Even the small island of Agalega caught their attention, mainly because we came within forty miles of its shores. For some reason they seemed to imagine that every island in the Indian Ocean, however small or barren, had a restaurant and a supermarket stacked high with supplies of fresh food. All we could see on the chart was a large coconut plantation, a boathouse and a jetty.

With seven hundred miles to go we prepared for stronger winds and bigger seas. Some of the waves now rolling up behind *Phoenicia* were six metres high, but I knew we could expect even larger as we headed towards Madagascar. A couple of the brailing lines had broken again but we couldn't replace them without taking the mainsail down. With the other brailing lines working we decided this was not a major concern and we left them in place.

Now our dramatic progress was interspersed with periods of light winds, rain and thunderstorms. We gave a wide berth to the tip of Madagascar, Cape d'Ambre, where two currents converge with the prevailing southeasterly winds, often causing confused and angry seas. As we headed to Mayotte we would have to pass between an island and a reef before we could make our final approach.

With a few days to go before we reached land *Phoenicia* had a chance encounter with a Syrian ship, *Aboudi V*. She had come from Socotra in Yemen and was on the same course as *Phoenicia* as she headed towards Mozambique. Most of the crew came from Arwad and it gave them their first chance to see the ship under sail. Mohamad Osman, the ship's owner and a generous sponsor of the expedition, kindly agreed to provide some food supplies. We had been at sea for six weeks and we were running low on many items by this point. The rice was almost finished and I had rationed the pasta and noodles to a couple of packs a day to ensure we had some carbohydrates with our meals for the rest of the trip.

However, as we came to make the exchange it was clear the swell would make the transfer between our vessels too dangerous. We had come mouth-wateringly close to replenishing our supplies and enjoying a tasty meal of chicken and rice, and the disappointment only compounded the crew's frustrations further. I consoled them with the news that we were less than two hundred miles from our destination. Unfortunately, soon afterwards the wind died and landfall began to seem a much greater distance away. It took another two days for the winds to pick up again.

As we approached the reef that surrounded the island we lowered the mainsail and carefully made our way through the entrance passage to Mayotte. From beneath the waves a magnificent pod of dolphins emerged to escort us, gently coaxing *Phoenicia* towards her destination. The reef passage was ten miles long and as we made our way in, the sun began to set in a blaze of orange and pink. It was dark by the time we anchored but we had reached land at last, after six and a half weeks of sailing.

13

The island of Mayotte was a welcome sight after so long at sea. Strictly speaking it is one of two islands lying close together and we had arrived at the smaller of the two. Perched near the northwest tip of Madagascar, Mayotte makes up one of four in an archipelago known as the Comoros. The rest have gained independence while Mayotte remains a remote French territory, a complex mix of French laws and systems but ethnically and culturally tied to the others. Conveniently for us this tiny island had an airport linking it to the rest of the world.

We anchored in the beautiful clear waters on Mayotte's western side and I went ashore to sort out the paperwork so the crew could disembark. Unluckily for the Omanis I discovered they would need visas to leave *Phoenicia*, even if this was just to get to the airport. It would take a few days to arrange and they would be confined to the ship in the meantime. They were desperate to leave and the news was not well received. In the end I wasted two days trying to sort out visas before the French authorities relented. Their flights were booked and they made their way home, which did much to diminish the stress on board.

For the rest of us it was an opportunity to take it easy and unwind. The French ex-patriot community was welcoming and helpful and we availed ourselves of their yacht club facilities. It was sheer indulgence to be able to relax, enjoy ice-cold drinks and fresh food, and get the chance to wash away the salt ingrained in every pore.

I was relieved to find that the deviation to our route had not appeared to deter anyone from finding our new destination. Nick Swallow returned to participate in a second leg and Keith Johnson flew in from Florida to join us. He was in his mid-fifties and found *Phoenicia*'s appeal in his fascination for ancient civilisations, whereas Daniel Hallstrom and Alice Palmer, a young couple from North Carolina, had come looking for adventure. Steph Edwards made up the last of the new recruits. She was British, the youngest at only twenty-five, and she had a pleasant easy-going manner. I was optimistic there would be a more relaxed atmosphere on the next leg and with a week until we sailed again we had an opportunity to get to know each other. It also gave the new crew a chance to adjust to life on board before the realities of Phoenician sailing set in. We used the time to explore our surroundings and discovered a shop along the airport road where we could buy provisions. After this we ventured into Mayotte's lush green interior, but the majority of our stay was spent by the warm azure waters where we could snorkel among the coral reefs and swim with turtles.

As the week drew to a close we began to prepare for our departure. The morning before we left we were about to go ashore to pick up some supplies when Dirman discovered a problem.

'Boss, boss,' he called out as he leant over the side, 'boat gone.'

The dinghy had been floating in the water, tied to the ship, but now the rope hung limply against *Phoenicia*'s hull; its charge had vanished. The nights had been pleasantly warm and most of the crew had been sleeping on deck, but not one of us had woken as thieves had made their way out to *Phoenicia*, cut the rope and stolen the dinghy. We were stranded.

I phoned the yacht club and Pierre, a young Frenchman who worked there, came out to take me ashore so I could report the theft to the police. Pierre spent the rest of the day ferrying us back and forth, allowing us to take on all the provisions we needed before we left. Later that day the police brought back our inflatable, which had been found in a nearby mangrove swamp. The outboard motor had been removed and the inflatable abandoned, slashed beyond repair. I managed to buy a tender from another contact we had made and although this delayed us for a couple of days, a huge effort from the crew and a large dose of kindness from the locals prevented it from taking any longer.

Two days before Christmas we weighed anchor and began negotiating our passage through Mayotte's reef. We had timed our departure to when the falling tide emptied the lagoon into the Indian Ocean. This current gave us an encouraging nudge and by late evening we had cleared the reef. We raised the mainsail and headed south down the Mozambique Channel. My aim was to cross it as quickly as possible to reach the Mozambique current on the western side, which flowed south between October and February. However, in crossing the channel we had to pass through the heavy squalls and fierce electrical storms that lay in our path. Each one of these intense downpours drenched the deck and soon it began to leak. At times the water streamed into the cabin. We did our best to protect our bunks with plastic sheeting but inevitably they ended up soaked, as did much of our clothing. As soon as a bright spell emerged the ship would resemble a Chinese laundry, with items draped from every free line. The galley was suffering too; books and papers were curling from the damp and beads of water trickled down the electric wires. No one dared to touch them. Fortunately our main navigational equipment remained well protected and continued to function normally, although we became a little concerned about the possibility of lightning striking the ship. As frightening as storms like these must have been to the Phoenicians, the risk to electrical equipment was one worry they were spared. At night we watched spectacular storms ahead as flashes of lightning continually illuminated the horizon.

Despite the discomfort the new crew had settled in well, although Keith appeared to find the experience more physically demanding than perhaps he had expected. There was a good atmosphere on board and a fair amount of festive spirit when, two days after leaving Mayotte, we celebrated Christmas at sea. Our enjoyment of the day was tempered by foul weather, as each one of us took a drenching for an hour at the helm, but numerous Christmas treats were produced from the galley to keep us going. By the evening we had began to gather speed but we were still over forty miles from the south-flowing current.

Over the following days the rains eased and conditions improved. Dirman fixed a hole in the stern, which had caused the bilges to fill rapidly. It had become a constant battle trying to empty them and his repairs helped to lighten the workload. It wasn't until three days after Christmas that we reached the other side of the Mozambique Channel. Once we had found the current our speed picked up, but it brought with it some very strong winds and, at times, the ship was thrown around quite violently. The waves slammed into the beam and occasionally the bow, making *Phoenicia* shudder. Lying in my bunk I could feel the force of the water against the planks, knowing that was all there was separating me from the thunderous waves beyond.

By sailing further offshore we managed to avoid the worst of the winds, but at times we were pushed to within twenty miles of the rocky cliffs that ran along the shoreline. We made our way down the coast and past the delta of the mighty Zambesi river, where the current left us as it cut across the bay on a more direct route south. We continued to follow the line of the shore and by early morning on 3rd January we began our approach to Beira.

Negotiating the twelve-mile channel that leads to the port was a test of nerve. Timing is everything when entering Beira; with exceptionally strong tidal flows of up to six knots and a tidal range of six metres it was critical we entered the channel when it was in flood and well before high tide. It was only ten metres wide for much of its length and the sandbars along its course were frequently shifting. The buoys marking the channel were moved to reflect this, making our charts largely inaccurate. It took three hours to navigate, with more than a few anxious moments along the way.

We found our berth inside the harbour and Yuri's wife, Vera, was there to meet us. She had flown in from Brazil a few days earlier and had met up with Atzuko Senno, a young Japanese woman who was joining us until South Africa. Mozambique had been a Portuguese colony until 1975 so Vera had no trouble with the language and she smoothed our way, ensuring entry formalities could be handled quickly and efficiently. *Phoenicia*'s arrival had made it into the newspapers and the locals were delighted we had chosen to visit Beira rather than Maputo. Everyone was welcoming and friendly and a nearby restaurant owner was eager to show us why Mozambique is known for its food. With great generosity he provided us with a lavish welcome meal. It was a chance to indulge and we did, enjoying everything missing in our rather bland diet. We feasted on thick, juicy steaks smothered in hot pepper and chilli piri-piri sauce, chips, deep-fried calamari, fried pastry desserts and ice-cream, all washed down with cold South African beer.

I woke during the early hours of the morning in an ice-cold sweat with a searing pain tearing into my side. The rich food had stirred my ailing gall bladder. Not wanting to wake the rest of the crew I made my way off the boat and for hours I paced up and down the jetty clutching my ribs, hoping the agony would pass. I had been resisting the thought of going to hospital but by daylight I was forced to give in and called Yuri who was staying in a local hotel.

'Alô?,' a sleepy voice answered.

'Yuri it's Philip. I need your help. I have to see a doctor.'

'I'll be with you as soon as I can,' he replied.

Within half an hour we were on our way to a local emergency clinic. After a number of tests and a large dose of painkillers I was told to return later, but as the pain eased the urgency to deal with it eased too. I decided I would hold on and wait the couple of weeks it would take us to reach South Africa. I had no idea it was going to be harder to leave Beira than I had anticipated.

By the end of the week we were ready to start the next leg to Richards Bay. It was a heavy overcast day as we sailed down the channel, weaving our way between the sandbanks, but only an hour into the journey we hit a storm and the water became so rough that we were barely moving. Dirman was controlling the central rudder but as he came to turn the arm it suddenly came apart and the whole piece of metal fell away into the water. We moored by the side of the estuary and spent the night there before returning to the harbour the following morning. The rudder we had cobbled together in Port Sudan had given up and collapsed, and we would have to wait another week until a new one was ready.

When we left again it was five in the morning and this time the weather was calmer. Everything was going well, but as we negotiated the twists and turns of the twelve-mile channel I was gripped by another agonising bout of pain. I was finding it hard to stand and concentrating was impossible so I asked Yuri to take *Phoenicia* through the channel. I went below, lay on the cabin floor and waited for the pain to pass. This was an unnerving experience, not just for me but for the entire crew; the captain of their ship was lying below deck, unable to carry on. I promised to see a doctor as soon as we arrived at Richards Bay but we had to get there first.

Once out of the channel we headed into the Bay of Sofala and straight into a southerly headwind that kept trying to force us backwards. We needed to head as far east as possible to allow us to rejoin the Mozambique Current, about fifty miles off the coast, but for a week it remained elusive. With eleven of us I was operating a two-watch system, three four-hour watches during the day and two six-hour watches at night. While Sulhan, Aziz,

Yuri, Vera and Atsuko made up one watch, Dirman, Niklas, Alice, Daniel and Steph took the other. I was overseeing the ship and plotting our course.

The weather was fine and hot, the sun beat down on the deck and as we drifted along we spent much of the time trying to keep cool. This entailed moving around the ship, seeking the solace of the changing shadows, while straining to catch the wisp of a cooling breeze. Occasionally, when the sun became too intense to bear, some retreated to their bunks, despite it being the hottest and most uncomfortable place on board. With duty watches less taxing, the crew could relax and read or listen to music. Dirman was spotted more than once, borrowed iPod in hand, silently disco dancing his way around the deck. Sulhan could only look on, shaking his head in bewilderment.

With the increase in temperatures, showering became a far more frequent activity. With eleven of us a long queue would often form as the sun began to set. Washing on board *Phoenicia* required its own set of skills and a good sense of balance was crucial. As the ship rolled being able to stay upright and maintain some sort of dignity, while hovering precariously over an overhanging lavatory, was not always easy. Despite this, anyone who took too long could expect a loud tutting from Yuri's direction.

With several hours of warmth left in the day the crew could relax before dinner. On Saturdays and Wednesdays we gathered on deck for happy hour, which had become markedly happier with the addition of the alcohol we had acquired in Beira. Adding this to our normal chocolate rations produced a potent sugar mix and animated conversations usually followed. Some would tell stories, while others talked about the day or discussed whatever topic came to mind. Aziz and Yuri both liked a good debate and while religion was guaranteed to fire up Aziz, Yuri could talk passionately on any subject relating to his country. As strict Muslims neither Sulhan nor Aziz drank alcohol; however, Dirman, liked the taste but was unwilling to drink in front of the other two. To overcome this problem he would hand me his Coke can and I would surreptitiously pour a small amount of beer into it. For the rest of the evening he would sit quietly, sip his beer and observe our antics, always with a huge smile on his face. Although he and Sulhan could only speak a few words of English, I suspected that by now they understood far more than they were prepared to let on.

While the days had been hot the nights were calm and time on deck had become an almost hypnotically peaceful experience. Hours could pass while listening to the lapping of the waves against the hull and the reassuringly familiar creaks and groans from the rigging. On the fourth night I had been getting some sleep below when I was woken by a hand on my shoulder.

'Philip, there's been an accident,' Yuri whispered.

Immediately I was wide awake.

'What's happened?' I asked.

'It's Atzuko, she's had a fall.'

I found her sitting on the galley floor, looking dazed and shocked; a cut above her lip was bleeding profusely. Vera had the first aid kit laid out in front of her and was trying to stem the flow. Atzuko had been leaving the helm when the ship had lurched unexpectedly to one side, throwing her tiny frame into the life raft. The cut was not serious but I was more concerned that she appeared to be slightly concussed. We made her lie down on the cabin floor while Vera spent the next few hours keeping a watch over her. Yuri returned to the deck and I tried to grab some more sleep.

At one in the morning a thunderous clattering shattered the peace and woke everyone asleep in the cabin. It was followed by Yuri's voice calling for all hands on deck. The starboard anchor had disappeared over the side and the deafening noise had been the heavy anchor chain rapidly unravelling behind it. Luckily Yuri had not been in the way when it had made its bid for freedom but he had had the presence of mind to secure the end before the full length of chain disappeared over the edge. The anchor had been rigged for easily release in case we had needed to stop suddenly when leaving Beira and, not having been strapped against the railings more securely out at sea, it had been working its way loose ever since. It took the entire crew nearly half an hour to pull in the twenty metres of heavy chain to recover the anchor. With peace restored the watch continued while the rest of us returned to our bunks.

Phoenicia may have been making slow and unspectacular progress but those on mother watch were determined the food would not be dull. With six different nationalities on board we were treated to a wide international menu. Atsuko's Japanese version of fish head soup was given the vote of approval, which is more than could be said for the Indonesian recipe. Niklas could be relied upon to turn out a good Swedish potato surprise at most mealtimes and despite regular threats from Aziz that we would be getting a meal of boiled water, great-tasting noodles usually appeared. Now puddings became a regular feature, although I was being very careful not to overindulge. Vera liked producing all sorts of sweets and biscuits, and bread or popcorn would appear to keep us going until dinner. Steph began to ingrain the habit of afternoon tea in the rest of the crew, having discovered what she described as a 'boat-proof' banana muffin recipe. However, the proudest moment for the English contingency was Daniel's conversion to the most quintessential taste of home – Marmite.

Despite the improvement in our meals tension had been building in the kitchen, with some of the women appearing to compete over how to run the galley. Vera made her disapproval known if she thought too much food was being prepared and then wasted. This was unfortunate for Alice who had trouble sleeping during the day and had been known to cook for hours while on mother watch.

At the beginning of the second week we picked up the Mozambique Current and the crew's focus switched to getting *Phoenicia* down the coast. As we headed towards Maputo and the border with South Africa the seas became bigger, the waves gathered to a height of six metres and *Phoenicia* began to lurch sideways. During the night the sail flapped violently until there was a loud ripping sound as five seams at the base of the canvas split open. Much of the following morning was spent repairing it under sail and while some of us anchored it tight with ropes, others used pliers to pull the needle and thread through the thick linen canvas. Each seam took over half an hour to mend but I was expecting stronger winds and it had to be done. We tightened the stays that supported the mast and I kept my fingers crossed the sail would hold. To my relief it remained intact and a few days later we completed the seven hundred mile leg, sailing into Richards Bay just before sunset.

15

The Zululand Yacht Club had been waiting for us and on our arrival over twenty yachts turned out to give us a characteristically warm South African reception. Kirsten, the Club's Commodore, and Charles, the Manager, were quick to offer us whatever help and support we might need. After my painful experience coming out of Beira one of my first questions was where I could find medical help. Fate was on my side as it turned out one of the members of the yacht club was a gastric surgeon. He was contacted immediately, the situation was explained to him and the next morning I was sitting in his consulting room.

I was offered further tests but it seemed pointless.

'Are you sure?' he asked.

I assured him that I was. I knew what was wrong and there was only one course of action.

'Then we can do it now if you want,' he replied.

He had already taken the precaution of booking an operating theatre and although I hadn't arrived expecting to go through the procedure that day I couldn't find a reason to wait; the quicker it was done the quicker I could recover and resume the expedition. I agreed, signed the forms and an hour later I was taken into theatre; two hours after that I was wheeled out again. Despite the considerable difficulties involved he had completed the operation using keyhole surgery. Thanks to his skill I had been spared a more extensive abdominal operation. This would have been the easier option for him but would have involved a much longer recovery time for me, and would have had a serious impact on the expedition.

'I've never seen a gall bladder as bad as yours,' he told me later, pointing out the huge risks I had taken by leaving it so long.

I recovered well and was out of hospital within two days. I stayed in a hotel overnight but during the day I was back on the ship, preparing her for the next leg and her greatest test so far: the Wild Coast and the Cape of Good Hope.

While I had been in hospital *Phoenicia* had been on the yacht club's slipway undergoing her own operation. With her stern jacked up, the frame supporting the prop shaft and central rudder was replaced and she received a new coat of pine tar. Meanwhile the crew had made repairs to the split in the sail. The club had been looking after everyone well and there had been a welcome party in my absence. They hosted numerous gatherings for us during our two-week stay and we met many club members, most of whom were fascinated to know more about the ship and our journey. One, Len Helfrich, a sailor and adventurer, generously gave up hours of his spare time to help with engine repairs and maintenance. He was an inspirational character, with a vast knowledge of boats and how to fix them, and I was delighted when he agreed to join the expedition to Durban. It was the start of his love affair with *Phoenicia* and in the end he remained with us until Cape Town.

Another member with a passion for sailing was Peter Hickman. His spare time was consumed with rebuilding his own yacht and although he had never been outside Africa he wanted to explore the seas with his wife, Vanessa. He attended every party and was never short of anything to say; if he wasn't telling a story he was asking a question and by the time we were ready to leave he had discussed the journey at length with a number of the crew. On our last evening in Richards Bay the club organised a final *braai* in our honour and we got a chance to say goodbye and thank all those who had helped us so generously during our stay.

As the evening was beginning to wind down, Peter came to find me.

'So, do you think I can join you?' he asked.

I had been expecting the question for days but had wondered if he was ever going to get around to asking it. He was overflowing with enthusiasm and life was never going to be dull with him on board so I agreed.

He grinned, 'That's lekker,' he replied, which was apparently a good thing.

The following morning he showed up on time with a bag packed, fishing gear in hand and a smile on his face. Karim Khwanda completed the line up. He was a Syrian who had travelled from Damascus to join *Phoenicia* and being bright, likeable and enthusiastic, he was another refreshing injection of energy for the team.

Having negotiated the entrance to the harbour at Richards Bay two weeks earlier I knew it would be a difficult exit. We had to make our way out of the east-facing channel and into a headwind before we could get out into the ocean again. We furled the sail as far up the yard as it would go, but even with the engine assisting us we were getting slower and slower. Dirman was on the rudder but it didn't seem to be responding and as we headed out I could feel something wasn't right. A check on our position made it clear in which direction we were going – we were being blown backwards and *Phoenicia* was gradually inching her way towards the harbour wall. The two boats escorting us out could do nothing to help. Momentarily I wondered if I should drop anchor or return to the yacht club, but a few seconds later I gave the order to bring down the yard. Although the sail was furled there must have been enough still showing to catch the wind and push us in the wrong direction. As the yard dropped to the deck we began to edge away from the wall and out of the harbour mouth. *Phoenicia* was a difficult ship to handle but I was beginning to get used to her idiosyncrasies.

We headed into the fresh winds and choppy seas. A large, orange sun was melting into the horizon as *Phoenicia*'s purple and white sail puffed out in the wind. We found the current very quickly and soon we were making rapid progress. We averaged five knots in perfect weather conditions assisted by a fresh north-easterly wind, relatively moderate seas and the Agulhas Current. We were in Durban eighteen hours later after completing the shortest leg so far.

It was early morning when we began our approach to Durban harbour. The wind was still blowing on our arrival and even with the sail almost completely reefed to slow us down we were still doing over five knots. Steph and Daniel were working the helm as we guided *Phoenicia* into the busy port entrance. It was going smoothly until a large cargo ship appeared from behind, forcing us over to the far starboard side of the channel. Moving slowly, we lost steerage and *Phoenicia* began to head towards a very large metal marker buoy. As it came closer we made desperate attempts to avoid a collision. While Dirman and Sulhan shouted out instructions in Indonesian, incomprehensible to most of the crew, the rest of us were pulling, climbing, pushing and valiantly battling with the buoy. Marina staff were on hand to help but this only seemed to add to the confusion. Eventually our efforts paid off and *Phoenicia* just managed to scrape past it leaving her signature, a streak of pine tar, as she went. We were lucky to escape with only minor damage to the heads.

I knew it would be a week before there was another window of good weather, which gave the crew time for a break. We had been alerted to the high crime levels in Durban and the need to be vigilant, but we were soon exploring the museums, the noisy and colourful outdoor markets, and the beautiful botanic gardens. There was a sense of excitement everywhere we went as South Africa prepared to host the football World Cup.

Some of the crew decided to get away from the city and ventured out into the countryside for a few days of camping in the mountains. The rest of us stayed on board to welcome a stream of visitors who wanted to see the ship.

One night during our stay Durban harbour was rocked by a

violent thunderstorm. I was standing at the doorway of the galley observing nature's angry display when I noticed the hatch on the deck starting to open. I caught the glint of a pair of eyes reflected in the light, then shortly afterwards wisps of smoke began rising from the opening. Sulhan was standing on the ladder while having a cigarette below deck. It was a dangerous choice of smoking venue and as an experienced sailor Sulhan knew that. Before thinking I shouted at him to put it out. The glow vanished and Sulhan disappeared, but I knew immediately that I had handled the situation badly. The following day he did his best to avoid me, glancing away rather than making eye contact. That evening I realised the depth of his feeling when I found a waterproof jacket I had lent him for the journey neatly laid out on my bunk. I asked Aziz to talk to him but I already knew that Sulhan, being quiet and sensitive, had felt humiliated by the way I had reacted to his misdemeanour. I apologised for shouting and we made an uneasy truce. However, there was another issue Sulhan, Dirman and Aziz wanted to address and this was far more serious.

The four of us sat down at a table outside the marina office. Aziz acted as spokesman and translator for the other two, who seemed more than a little agitated. He explained the problem: there were two couples on board and some bunk sharing had started to creep in. Surprisingly, despite being the most religious and radical of the three, Aziz was more conciliatory than the others. He had been university educated and this had given him more exposure to western ideas. Sulhan was particularly upset, even though Aziz had persuaded him that Daniel and Alice were married. It was not just that any contact between the sexes before marriage was a religious taboo, it was seen as a very bad omen; their belief in traditional island superstitions had convinced them that this behaviour would bring misfortune to *Phoenicia* and her crew. Such was the strength of their feelings on the matter that all three informed me they intended to leave if it happened again. I couldn't afford to lose them and I assured Aziz I would deal with it. I persuaded them to come as far as Cape Town, where we would review the situation again. Fortunately my reassurances, and the offer of a bonus to carry on to the end of the expedition, seemed to have the desired effect.

By the time the crew who had been camping returned they found we had another Phoenician convert. One of the visitors to the ship was a young New Zealand sports coach working in East London. Tony Lambdon was a triathlete and had the energy and fitness levels that would make him an asset to the crew.

The weather complied with our plans and *Phoenicia* set sail for the two hundred and fifty-mile push to East London. We raised the sail a mile from the breakwater, once again seeking out the Aghulhas Current. Fourteen miles off the coast we struck gold and for much of the night we sped along at five knots, but by morning a low-pressure system had swept through our route, bringing with it strong southwesterly winds that whipped up the waves. I knew we were in for a bumpy ride and with a hundred and eighty miles still to go we were running out of time; the weather was forecast to turn against us within forty-eight hours and the change would have pushed *Phoenicia* back up the coast towards Durban. Thankfully the winds picked up and, with assistance from the current, we began to race along at eight knots, a speed I never thought *Phoenicia* would reach.

As we contended with the weather, Len was kept busy dealing with technical failures. The compass and tricolour mast lights stopped working and although he managed to fix the worn out wires on the compass light, the answer to the problem with the navigation lights lay at the top of the mast. No one wanted to investigate a problem so high above our heads when seven-metre waves were buffeting *Phoenicia* from side to side. As the second set of navigation lights remained operational we could manage, but a tear in the sail was a much more serious problem. It had been re-stitched in Richards Bay but one seam must have been missed and as we battled the winds it had opened up, widening to a large, gaping two-metre hole. We were left with no choice; it had to be repaired, which meant lowering the sail and stitching the seam. At times the effort resembled a rugby scrum with Daniel, Yuri and Tony trying to hold the sail on the deck, while Peter and Dirman did their best to apply the stitches.

The last night was *Phoenicia*'s most impressive performance. The miles seemed to evaporate as she surfed down mountainous waves to record a phenomenal, current-assisted speed of ten and a half knots. For an ancient ship this was verging on supersonic. We were going so fast that as we approached East London we had to pull out all the stops to slow down. We waited, drifting outside the harbour as a ship left the narrow entrance, before we made our way up the channel. Until there was another weather window later in the week we could rest, make repairs and contemplate our approach to the Cape.

16

The brevity of our stay did nothing to diminish the warmth of our welcome and as we entered the harbour at the mouth of the Buffalo River a small flotilla of yachts was waiting to greet us. East London is better known for its commercial port, but there are two yacht clubs within the marina at Latimer's Landing and both gave us a great reception. Although I intended it to be a short stop we needed to make a few repairs. It had also been a physically demanding leg and the crew had worked hard so we were grateful for the opportunity to get a decent night's sleep. As we spent time trying to sort out a fuel problem with the engine we received news that Tony, who had briefly left the ship to see some friends, had been involved in a car accident on his way back. Unhurt but badly shaken, he had decided it would be better if he rejoined us further down the coast and with some doubts about the weather I decided to postpone sailing until the following day.

We departed from Latimer's Landing on a grey morning, shrouded in mist and light drizzle. This didn't seem to hamper our progress and by midday we were already six miles off the coast and reaching speeds of six knots. Despite a generator failure during the night, which reduced us to emergency power, by the next morning we were closing in on our destination. A hundred and twenty miles had taken just thirty-six hours.

We sailed into Algoa Bay in Port Elizabeth to another enthusiastic welcome. *Phoenicia*'s appearance created quite a stir and cannon fire echoed across the bay as we approached. A launch heaved with photographers and film crew who were awaiting our arrival, and once we had disembarked a press conference followed. We were given a mooring at the Algoa Yacht Club, where only five months earlier a ferocious storm had washed away every berth.

In less than forty-eight hours we had repaired the sail, mended the generator and even found time to go on a short safari, generously donated by a nearby private game reserve. It would have been a pleasure to stay longer but there was a weather window that looked too good to miss. Tony had rejoined the ship and three more South Africans, John Glenister, Justin Bean and Clinton Clements had fallen under *Phoenicia*'s spell. Clinton had been working at the game reserve when we met him, but it turned out he was a genuine cowboy, having learnt his skills in South America. He had an interest in Viking voyages and an ambition to participate in one but this expedition seemed to be a good enough substitute. Our crew numbers had risen to fifteen. Perhaps it was the chance to make history that was proving so popular, although I suspected it was more likely to be the thrill of the dangers involved in attempting to round the Cape.

We sailed out of Algoa Bay in search of the Agulhas Current once again. The conditions were in our favour, but even if the weather drastically changed I knew we could take shelter in Mossel Bay, halfway to our destination; if it stayed fair we had a chance to round the Cape. Once we had found the current our pace quickened. This lasted for a couple of days before we parted company and the current divided in two, one branch heading north and the remainder south, before it curled back across the Indian Ocean. Strong winds were forecast and I felt it was too good an opportunity to miss so I decided to have a shot at getting round the Cape in one go. I hoped the forecast was right, as once we had passed Mossel Bay there were no bolt-holes to run to if the weather turned nasty. This had the potential to be the most risky part of our entire circumnavigation of Africa.

We slowed for a couple of days while we waited for stronger winds. There was a noticeable drop in temperature and for once it was comforting to get into a warm bunk below deck. We discovered Clinton shared Peter's love of fishing and they would spend hours swapping angling stories while catching our supper.

It transformed our fishing successes and in one morning they managed to haul in three, the last a huge yellow fin tuna. Even with fifteen on board we were not going to go hungry.

When the strong winds arrived there was no more time for fishing and, as the gusts backed to the southeast, we reset the sail and sped up to over five knots. As the night progressed the wind increased further. By now we had reached the Agulhas Bank and were approaching the southernmost tip of Africa, where the warm Indian Ocean and the cool Atlantic currents meet, often a confused and turbulent marriage. We negotiated our way past the oil and gas platforms, while keeping an eye on the oncoming shipping lane. We passed by uneventfully and under control and by four-thirty in the morning we were racing along at six knots. I was on deck with the early morning watch when suddenly a loud ripping sound silenced the crew. Everyone's gaze turned skyward as the purple and white mainsail divided in two before our eyes. A weak seam had ripped apart and we were left staring in shock and amazement at the two pieces of canvas that were flailing against the mast.

The sail was useless and we needed to get it down as quickly as possible. In strong winds and heavy seas this was a difficult and dangerous manoeuvre and I needed all fifteen crew on deck. There was just enough light for us to see as we brought the storm sail up from below and attached it to a shortened yard, stowed alongside the cabin. We re-rigged the tacks, braces and sheets as fast as we could, then we got into position and with a quick and rhythmic effort furled up the sail as far as it would go before lowering the yard. Once the sail was down we were at the mercy of the elements in an area renowned for its treacherous and unpredictable sailing conditions. A large wave or gust of wind could have turned us broadside and then we risked capsizing. As we hoisted the storm sail one of the sheets got twisted, flapping violently until we had brought it under control. The whole operation took the best part of an hour and during this time we had been slowly drifting closer and closer to the edge of the shipping lane. Just as we finished two vessels emerged from the mist far closer to us than I would have liked, but we were back in control with the storm sail aloft and out of immediate danger.

The conditions we encountered the following day made me grateful the sail had not ripped any later. By this point gale force winds and powerful seven-metre seas had turned our passage into a white-knuckle ride. We covered a breathtaking distance of a hundred and fifty miles in twenty-four hours, a record for *Phoenicia*. During the night the swell was so strong that we had to climb onto the cabin roof to be able to pick out the shipping heading our way. At times three people were needed on the helm to hold our course as we cut through the water at seven knots. Occasionally a large wave would smash over the deck, drenching everyone in its way. Weatherboards prevented water coming into the cabin and fortunately no one was washed off their feet, but all of us got a thorough cold water soaking. Going to the heads became a rather traumatic experience. Standing on a small wooden platform overhanging the ship, while being thrown around by the ferocious seas below was a test of mettle. We placed our lives in the hands of Dirman's carpentry and prayed.

In the early hours of the morning we passed the Cape of Good Hope. It was an incredible feeling – not only had we rounded the Cape but we had done it in a reconstruction of a Phoenician vessel. Had a ship bearing a horse's head achieved the same feat two and a half thousand years earlier? If so had they known the significance of what they had done? This little wooden ship was being battered by the wind and the waves but she had valiantly pushed on, showing us she could handle these difficult and dangerous seas. I couldn't prove that the Phoenicians had taken this journey, but I had proved their ships were more than capable of the task. It was a proud moment for me, for the crew and for all those who believed in *Phoenicia*.

However, before we could celebrate our achievement we

faced the challenge of being able was to slow down sufficiently to enter Table Bay. The conditions were not letting up and with southeasterly winds pushing up to thirty knots it was not going to be easy. As the wind curled round the Cape I knew I needed to negotiate a particular line to stand a chance of getting in: if I came in too close to the coast *Phoenicia* risked losing the wind completely, but too far out and we could get blown further into the Atlantic. Fortunately it went without a hitch and when we approached the lee of Table Mountain the winds dropped enough for us to sail almost effortlessly into Table Bay. As we sailed down the narrow channel to the Victoria and Albert Waterfront, the passenger bridge was raised to let us in. Onlookers began to form a line on both sides of the quay, almost within touching distance. Suddenly and spontaneously they began to clap as we passed by.

17

As the adrenalin subsided exhaustion took over. Safely alongside in Cape Town with Table Mountain as our backdrop, we could relax and reflect on what we had achieved. It had been an incredible six days of sailing and many of the crew felt they had taken part in a once-in-a-lifetime experience. Alice flew out from the UK to join us and she found it hard to believe how different the ship looked since leaving Syria in August 2008. *Phoenicia* had certainly weathered and darkened in colour and in some way, like those who had travelled with her, she seemed a little stronger and wiser. We had been through her experiences, both good and bad, and we were learning with her.

Our little wooden ship made an interesting and unusual sight lined up alongside the graceful and sleek lines of the modern fibreglass yachts. One was a seventeen metre Indian navy sailing vessel called *Mhadei* whose captain, Commander Dilip Dhonde, was attempting to become the first Indian to circumnavigate the world. He was nearly seven months into his journey and about to set off on his final and longest leg. However, even this modern yacht was dwarfed by a thirty-metre Arabian trimaran called *Majan*. She was a sleek racing machine, incorporating the latest developments in technology and design, making her lightweight and super fast. When her two Omani crew invited me to come aboard I felt as if I had stepped into another world. Despite the obvious differences in our styles of boat we had much common ground: we were learning to deal with punishing seas, unpredictable and violent weather conditions, the vagaries of the winds and currents, and above all, we wanted a safe and successful conclusion to our journeys.

Phoenicia attracted plenty of attention and we began to run daily tours of the ship. Peter was a willing guide and his enthusiasm, knowledge and ability to talk at length made him the perfect choice. Other crew also took tours and answered questions, each able to give their individual perspective on what they had experienced. Surprisingly, many visitors showed a real understanding of Phoenician history and plenty of locals keenly agreed with our theory that the Phoenicians could have been the first people to circumnavigate Africa, gracing South Africa's shores long before Bartolomeu Dias in 1488. Unfortunately some of the stories were either unsubstantiated or inaccurate. A number of visitors believed Phoenician beads had been found along the coast. I had come across this information before the expedition and an academic had assured me the beads were of a much later date and of Portuguese origin, having been used by some of the first cattle traders as a form of bartering. Others had intriguing tales of Phoenician shipwrecks, allegedly discovered in South African waters, although to my knowledge no hard evidence of these wrecks exists.

One piece of information was far more interesting and potentially of much greater significance. I was given pictures of Roman coins, which had been identified as coming from Alexandria in the 4th century AD. They had been found near the Cape and were in good condition, which made it possible that they had lain undiscovered since that time. If it is plausible that the Romans had made it round the Cape of Good Hope by this date, I believe it is not unreasonable to think the Phoenicians could have done the same a thousand years earlier, given the marginal differences in sailing technology available to them.

During our stay most of the crew seemed reluctant to part with their trusted friend and continued to rough it on board. The ship had become part of each of us and we had got used to living by the natural rhythms we had at sea. We took turns keeping an eye on the ship, cooking together and sleeping in various patterns throughout the day and night, which was not always easy when a group of noisy seals spent their time lounging around on the jetty, grunting and barking at regular intervals.

Aside from giving history lessons on the Phoenicians, everybody worked very hard on getting the ship ready for the next leg at sea. The purple and white mainsail that had ripped so spectacularly during our passage around the Cape was mended and Sulhan tackled the leaking deck by methodically ridding it of its old caulking and replacing it with a new, waterproof version. I hoped that from now on when it rained there would be no accompanying downpour below deck, but just in case the caulking failed we carefully stapled plastic sheeting around our bunks and belongings to keep them as dry as possible.

A number of the crew spent days after we arrived working on the engine and fitting new water pumps. Len worked particularly hard on these repairs, donning his overalls every day and disappearing into his 'office' as he liked to call it. He had come to the end of his sailing with us but only because his passport had expired. We were going to miss him but he was not the only member of crew leaving. John and Justin were also remaining in South Africa and once we got into harbour John rushed off to his daughter's wedding, which was taking place the following day. She had been philosophical about the prospect of her father missing her big day. 'Don't worry I can get married again but this is a once-in-a-lifetime chance to sail around the Cape,' she had told him.

Tony went back to work in East London and Vera returned to Brazil. Clinton had taken to the experience and decided to stay but Peter flew back home to Richards Bay. We had a feeling we would see him again and a week later he reappeared accompanied by his wife, Vanessa, giving us a crew of eleven for the next leg.

Before we left a group effort ensured we had enough food stocks for around ninety days at sea. Our next three stops were the remote Atlantic islands of St Helena, Ascension and the Azores where I knew supplies would be expensive and difficult to find. After a few large shopping sprees I looked at the piles of boxes stacked on the dock and wondered where we were going to put everything. It became a test of innovation to find storage space, but each item was reorganised, stacked and then crammed into any nook we could find. Eventually we managed to locate a place for every box, bag and can.

Not every day of our stay entailed hard work. We found time to climb Table Mountain, visit Cape Point, enjoy a tour of the Delheim wine estate in Stellenbosch*, watch the penguins waddle up Boulders Beach and take in a sunset cruise on the tourist pirate ship *Jolly Roger*. On our last night Alice had arranged a gala evening with the Royal Cape Yacht Club. The Syrian Ambassador to South Africa and members of the Indonesian Consulate were there to wish us well. It was a great way for us to end our stay and a chance for me to thank the many generous people who had helped us during our visit.

We left Cape Town on 21st March. It was a busy Sunday afternoon as tourists and shoppers wandered around the quayside. Yuri and I discussed the logistics of leaving and whether we should warn the port officials of our departure. To get out of the marina we had to go through a narrow channel spanned by a drawbridge, which allowed people to walk from one side of the quay to the other. It would rise just enough to allow the mast of a vessel to pass through.

'Don't worry,' Yuri reassured me, 'They do this all the time, they'll raise the bridge when they see us coming.'

This is what had happened on our arrival and as the whole process had been smooth and efficient there was no reason to think our exit would be any different. We cast off and began to head down the channel while the tourists watched us from the bridge, but as *Phoenicia*'s fifty-tonne frame began building up momentum they continued to watch, the bridge stayed firmly closed and I realised we were going to have to stop rapidly before our mast slammed straight into it. I put the engine in reverse, or what

*The Delheim Estate was a generous sponsor of the expedition

I thought was reverse, only to find we were still going forwards. I had missed the gear and I quickly tried again, yanking the lever firmly into place. This time we made a *Phoenicia*-style emergency stop.

I was furious; we had little room for error and now we would have to manoeuvre *Phoenicia*'s heavy bulk from a standing start. It took ten minutes for the bridge to be raised, by which time the ranting of an irate Phoenician captain had turned the air a deep shade of blue. Fortunately, in the end, it worked smoothly and the weekend crowds watched us sail out of the Victoria and Albert Waterfront escorted by seals, a few boats and the *Jolly Roger* pirate ship.

It was good to be back out at sea again. The miles clocked up quickly over the first few days as we headed northwards up the coast of West Africa, assisted by a southerly breeze and the Benguela Current. The sky was blue and the ocean jade green, but the temperature had dropped significantly and the first few nights were bitterly cold. After spending a chilly six hours on watch we were forced to retreat to our bunks in most of our clothes. The crew had spent much time in South Africa waterproofing and improving their sleeping quarters. Now they were covered with blankets and plastic sheeting, while some were even adorned with curtains and pockets. Steph had made her bunk into such a cosy nest that the rest of us worried we would never get her out of it again.

At times the sea became so choppy two people were needed to take the helm as *Phoenicia* became too lively for one to control. After a few days we began to leave the coast and head further into the Atlantic, following the prevailing winds and currents. However, by the fourth day these winds had dropped and we began more of a drift towards the tiny island of St Helena. Thankfully the air began to warm, although the sea remained freezing cold, with the Benguela Current bringing deep ocean waters to the surface. Showering was no longer a popular activity; standing in the heads and dowsing with sea water that had come from the icy depths was a distinctly unappealing prospect. While most found a myriad of reasons to avoid it Clinton seemed to relish the experience. As the days went by the thought of the crew not washing until our next stop was too unpleasant a prospect to contemplate, both for us and the poor islanders of St Helena. Fortunately after a quick search of the cabin I managed to dig out a solar shower, which I laid on the deck to warm up.

During the journey Peter and Clinton carried on sharing their fishing stories and putting out lines, while landing increasing numbers of tuna. As we moved away from the shallow waters of the continental shelf there were fewer sea birds but sharks became more frequent visitors. When we spotted two fins slowly cruising down our starboard side we had a good idea from their size what must have been lurking under the water. Later we managed to catch a smaller one, just over a metre in length, and a tussle ensued trying to get it on deck. Daniel cleaned, gutted and filleted our catch while Alice added some herbs. She had created a thriving herb garden in an array of buckets, which were displayed on the cabin roof. The shark made a delicious supper, much softer than we had expected and with a similar taste to Dover sole. An even larger one took the line a few days after this, but it was given clemency and released after Clinton delicately pulled the lure from its tooth-filled jaws.

As usual Dirman spent much of his time pacing the ship seeking out any repairs and mechanical jobs he could find. We had noticed a diesel leak around the generator only to discover the fuel filter unit had broken, but before I could ask for help Dirman had taken the whole unit off and had plumbed in a new one. On completion of this task he turned his attention to the fire hose, which had started to leak after eighteen months of wear. He had an amazing knack of knowing where to find everything on board, down to the smallest component, and not long after he had located a piece of plastic hosepipe and a couple of jubilee clips we had a new fire hose. Whatever task Dirman was tackling he did it with good humour and it was a joy to be around him.

Despite our slow pace, we were gradually moving northwest, pushing away from the Namibian coast and out of the major shipping lanes. By the end of the first week at sea we had set a course heading directly for St Helena, still over one thousand two hundred miles away. It had become rare to see any other ships, although we did spot one fishing boat; it came to within five hundred metres so their crew could check out the strange vessel they had spotted bobbing along in the water. Alone in the ocean for much of the time, any signs of life became the cause of great excitement and a call of 'look at this' usually prompted a rush for cameras as we hung over the side to get a better look. When a massive five-foot turtle stretched out its head to see us passing in front of it there was an audible gasp from the crew.

By the time we were halfway to St Helena the sea had turned a royal blue and the water had become slightly warmer. Thankfully it was no longer necessary to go to sleep in all the clothes we possessed, now just a few layers sufficed, but a sunny spot on deck remained a much-coveted piece of territory. Once the ship was on a fairly consistent course there was usually only the occasional sail tweaking to tax us and on some nights it was so quiet and peaceful the only sounds were the gentle whirr of the wind generator, the slosh of the swell rolling past and *Phoenicia*'s familiar creaks and groans.

During a quiet watch the one challenge that faced us was what form of entertainment to choose. Most of the crew had become prolific readers with nearly everyone bringing a few books with them. This ensured the ship's library had an interesting variety of texts to choose from, although some were distinctly more high-brow than others, ranging from sailing books and essays about Islam to crime and historical romance. The most popular spot for these activities was sitting on the spare yard on the starboard side of the ship, which doubled up as a smoking bench. It was here that Peter, Dirman and Sulhan could frequently be spotted, puffing away contentedly while staring out to sea. Others found unique ways to entertain their fellow crew mates and at times Clinton would amuse us by transforming *Phoenicia* into Noah's ark. He was a natural mimic and when he delved into his repertoire, a menagerie of animals and birds would come to life as the sounds of the bush dispersed across the ocean. If we wanted music Yuri could produce a tune on his recorder and Daniel was known to burst into spontaneous bouts of singing, especially when at the helm. With an Indonesian language CD on board the crew made efforts to converse and joke with Sulhan and Dirman in their native tongue, with varying degrees of success.

The evening meal was usually the most sociable part of the day, when the galley would fill with people reading, writing, playing games of chess or cards, or using the laptop to send our daily blogs. Often someone would be checking how many miles we had travelled and how many we still had to go, as there was always a friendly wager on the number of days it would take to get to our next port.

We were within seven hundred miles of our destination when our pace began to pick up, but now the weather and the sea became much more erratic. We moved from heavy grey clouds to bright blue skies then back to gloom again. There were times when a big wave would roll towards us and hit *Phoenicia* with such force that it would lift her out of the water, then plunge her back down with a thud seconds later.

By 1st April we were still at sea and a mischievous crew were not going to let the day pass unnoticed. Complaining that the stove was not working properly, Yuri presented everyone with sachets of instant noodles for lunch. Never known to get flustered or to grumble Steph simply shrugged her shoulders and started to open a packet. Meanwhile Alice, Daniel and I had decided to make some alterations to the fishing equipment, fastening an old blue plastic jug to one of the lines. The added drag, caused by the weight of the jug, stretched out the line to simulate a rather large fish. When Clinton emerged on deck for the on-coming shift he immediately noticed the taut line. Barely able to contain his excitement he gave it a sharp tug.

'We've caught a fish and it's a big one,' he shouted.

'What sort of fish is it?' Yuri demanded to know.

'It's a dorado … no … hang on … it's blue. I don't know what kind of fish it is but it's a big blue one.'

His exuberance stopped abruptly once he realised he was reeling in a big plastic bucket, to shrieks of laughter from the others.

The unpredictable weather continued with a brace of rain squalls and sudden wind shifts. Although the swell occasionally brought a wave crashing on deck we kept at a steady pace and five days later, with shouts of 'Land Ahoy' from Clinton, we sighted the rocky outline of St Helena's eastern side. Aziz had won the bet: we had been at sea for seventeen days.

It was cold and drizzling as we anchored off Jamestown. Large grey clouds of mist swirled around us, deadening the sounds and creating a strangely eerie atmosphere. St Helena's capital and only town was nestled into a steep-sided valley with lines of houses working their way down to the shore. From the ship we looked out over a rugged coastline with sheer volcanic cliffs dropping to the sea. A British overseas territory, the island lies squarely in the middle of the south Atlantic and in a place of only four thousand inhabitants, where everyone knows each other, we were bound to stand out as the crazy people on the strange wooden ship. However, the 'Saints', as the locals are known, were friendly and hospitable, although the accent took time to get used to. On our first day we were invited to the local radio station to tell our story, followed by an interesting phone interview with Sir Robin Knox-Johnston in the UK.

Only a small amount of provisioning was possible during our stay. Despite its tropical green slopes there is surprisingly little agriculture, and what is brought to market on Thursday mornings seems to cause a scrum among the normally laid-back population. With no airport the island has to rely on the Royal Mail ship, *St Helena*, for its supplies, so once we had bought a few essentials we had plenty of time to relax. Apart from spending hours fishing and swimming in the clear warm waters that surrounded the ship, the locals organised tours to show us around the island. This gave us the chance to visit the places lived in by their most infamous resident. Only St Helena was deemed remote enough for Napoleon's exile after the battle of Waterloo, and he remained there until his death six years later.

On our last day the yacht club gave us lunch, sending us off with stomachs full of fish *plo,* apparently short for pilau. This island recipe was a mix of rice, vegetables and fish, and Steph left armed with the recipe to add to the galley's repetoire. It was hard to tear ourselves away from the easy-going atmosphere on the island, but after a stay of six days it was time to make our way to our next island stop.

We had arrived in St Helena with a crew of eleven and left with eight after three unexpected departures. Alice had a job offer in the States that was too good to refuse and Yuri left to attend to some business matters but promised he would rejoin us in the Azores. Both hitched a lift on a yacht heading for Brazil. Although Peter was still keen to continue, his wife Vanessa was struggling with ill health and not altogether enamoured with the *Phoenicia* experience. She said an emotional goodbye to Peter and stayed in St Helena, where she had to wait another three weeks for the arrival of the Royal Mail ship to take her back to Cape Town.

Hauling up the anchor and hoisting the yard as we left gave us a sharp reminder of what hard work felt like. For all the extra effort it was still a revelation to find that fewer crew seemed to be able to do the same work as quickly and almost as efficiently as before. We left in our wake a view of St Helena's rocky silhouette bathed in warm April sunshine. The busy valley of Jamestown and the many houses perched above it gradually receded into the distance. It would be another seven hundred miles before we sighted land again.

Not long into the journey Clinton hauled in a huge dorado. Weighing more than thirty kilos and at well over a metre long it was a monster of a fish. It became a test of culinary imagination to try to create a new taste when the main ingredient remained the same for days. Dorado steaks, dorado soup, dorado pie and dorado fishcakes all followed in quick succession. Yuri was no longer on board to harangue the poor soul on mother watch to leave out the pepper, salt and chillies so our food had more flavour again. Aziz was particularly delighted to be able to return to a spicy menu and he resolved to make the most of every meal until Yuri's return. With enough fish supplies to keep us going I imposed a moratorium on angling activities, while we concentrated on other tasks.

Although the equator was still a thousand miles to our north, the trade winds were beginning to weaken. There was a noticeable increase in the temperature, but it remained cloudy and humid. No longer preoccupied with fishing, Clinton turned his attention to making a leather bag from a large piece of cowhide. Our resident cowboy had not only mastered cattle handling from the saddle but he was also accomplished at leatherwork, able to make his own bridles, saddles, bags and jackets. Naturally he became the expert for stitching and rope work on board and his technique for patching the sails was quick and efficient. Meanwhile Daniel filled notebooks with poems and sketches and Peter immersed himself in yachting manuals. He could often be found absorbed in his studies, poring over some aspect of navigation or safety as he worked his way towards his Yachtmaster's certificate. On his return to South Africa he intended to launch his own boat after years of painstaking work and repair.

After six days sailing we began our approach to Ascension but we were travelling at a speed of nearly six knots, which I knew would give us an arrival time around midnight. This was too late for us to anchor safely so we brailed up the sail to halve our speed. The RAF and US military both have a base on the island and from thirty miles away we could make out the bright lights of the airfield.

Ascension is another remote volcanic speck in the middle of the Atlantic ocean, forming part of the British Overseas Territory, which includes St Helena and Tristan da Cunha. It was first discovered at the beginning of the 16th century by the Portuguese, but not inhabited until 1815 when the British claimed ownership. Their motive was purely tactical: they feared their navy's arch-enemy, Napoleon, might be spirited away via this route. With no permanent residents, to this day it still holds military and strategic importance. In addition to the military bases the European Space Agency and a BBC transmitter, relaying the World Service to Africa, are housed on this tiny island. As a result, Ascension's population is made up of around a thousand transient workers.

In the morning we anchored off Georgetown, the capital and harbour, and one of only a handful of villages dotted around the island. We discovered that several locals had spotted us coming, as in modern times it is rare for ships to arrive under sail. The Island's administrator and Harbour Master were fascinated by *Phoenicia* so we gave them a tour of the ship.

Few people live in Georgetown and one of its only claims to fame is making it into the record books for having the worst golf course in the world. This is not surprising as it is made entirely from compacted lava. In fact much of Ascension looks like a moonscape, dotted with volcanic hills, craters and lava flows that have hardened into strange, contorted patterns. Place names like Two Boat Village, Cat Hill, Dead Man's Beach and Comfortless Cove conjured up images of children's adventure stories.

The island was once completely barren and George Forster, a member of Captain Cook's second voyage to the Pacific in 1775, described it as 'a ruinous heap of rocks'.[1] Sixty years later Darwin was equally unimpressed and wrote 'The island is entirely destitute of trees, in which, and in every other respect it is far inferior to St Helena.'[2] However, in the mid-nineteenth century, with the help of British botanists and a consignment of plants from Kew Gardens, a tropical forest known as Green Mountain was cultivated at its summit. We walked up to this man-made microclimate and wandered through the strange amalgamation of bamboo, fig, yew and palm trees, which sit under a permanent blanket of cloud. For all of us, though, the highlight of our stay was visiting the pristine white beaches lapped by deep blue water and framed by black volcanic rock flows. On our last day we went to Long Beach after dark so we could watch the green turtles. After hauling themselves over the sand with a Herculean effort, they spent the night digging pits in which to lay their eggs, before returning to the sea at dawn. It was rare to find such an isolated spot where nature was allowed to continue without interference from mankind and it was a moment to treasure during our short visit. Only three days after we had arrived we prepared to set sail again.

19

We left Ascension on 21ˢᵗ April knowing that we were facing our longest and potentially most challenging leg of the expedition. We had replenished our stocks of drinking water with enough to last us for sixty-five days and although the supply ship had not visited the island for over a month, we managed to get some meat and a few other items. We had more than enough dried provisions to last the journey.

It was a good start. The temperature was warm, the winds were strong and soon we were reaching speeds of six knots. I was grateful for as many days of good weather as I could get, knowing we were heading towards the Inter Tropical Convergence Zone. In the Atlantic this low-pressure area is more commonly known as the doldrums, when we could expect times of variable or even non-existent winds. In fact our luck held for four days until we were just over a hundred and twenty miles from the equator. At that point the trade winds that had carried us from Cape Town began to lose their strength.

Downpours became frequent, but the temperature remained high and it became hard to find respite from the oppressive heat and stickiness, both above and below deck. Like the wind, the crew's activities gradually slowed as the humidity sapped their energy. Some took time to catch up on studying or reading and when tuna began jumping from the water, fly-fishing became a popular pastime again. By dusk on one of our first evenings we had amassed two yellow fin tuna and half-a-dozen mackerel. It was a relaxing way to pass the hours while replenishing our supplies of fresh protein.

We fell back into the rhythm of the watch system. Divided into two groups of four, I was on Sulhan's watch alongside Daniel and Aziz, while Dirman took the other with Peter, Steph and

Clinton. The evening watch would begin at eight and each of us would take the helm for an hour, until the next team emerged for duty at two. Eight in the morning signalled the start of another watch, which allowed the others to head off to their bunks for some much needed sleep. The fourth member of each group would be on mother watch or 'on holiday', as the crew liked to call it. They would get a night's rest before waking early to prepare breakfast and do the rest of the day's cooking, cleaning and washing-up duties. This created the rhythm of our days and with weeks at sea we came to live and breathe this pattern.

Despite our slower pace, eight days after we left Ascension we had something to celebrate: in the early hours of the morning we crossed the equator after five and a half months in the southern hemisphere. King Neptune appeared again, looking suspiciously like Dirman, to perform a ceremony for those new to the experience. After Clinton, Daniel, Peter and Steph had endured a messy initiation involving eggs and a large quantity of water, we drank one of our prized bottles of wine, given to us by the Delheim Estate in Stellenbosch. It was a Grand Reserve 2004, the same year the expedition had been conceived and, aside from being an excellent wine, its opening marked a significant point in our voyage.

After this, one day seemed to flow into another as we continued our passage through the doldrums. To while away the hours some of the more adventurous took to jumping off the ship for a refreshing Atlantic swim. It was a pleasant way to cool down, although we were always careful to trail a long rope in case a sudden squall whipped up the wind without warning. As the humidity lingered both laundry activities and showering noticeably increased in frequency. A night in a Phoenician bunk could be an uncomfortably sweaty experience and with regular rain showers none of us had been bold enough to try sleeping on deck. Clothing, and particularly bedding, had begun to take on a curious scent. Steph eloquently summed up the aroma as 'a unique blend of rancid sweat, grease, fish, diesel, salt and pine tar'.

The crew knew they would be at sea for at least two months and this was a tough mental challenge. Floating on the ocean for weeks on end could have a strange effect on the most sane of sailors, and there were no opportunities to leave if the experience became too difficult. It was as much a test of mental as it was physical fitness. With the excitement of passing the equator gone, the point where we would have been coming to the end of a shorter leg coincided with drifting in the doldrums and the end of some of our fresh food, while the weather continued to hamper life on board. Dogged by near-constant wind changes and persistent showers, we seemed to be permanently in one of two states: either wet or in the process of drying out. Peter realised the rainwater wasn't his only problem when he discovered a large hole immediately below his bunk where the water was gushing in with every roll of the ship. He tried to stem the problem with plastic bags, but when this failed it elicited little sympathy from the rest of the crew. Eventually he moved bunks with much protesting and moaning.

To add to his woes, Peter had decided to give up smoking, along with a number of other crew members. As a result we left Ascension with very few packets on board, and gradually the cigarette cache was beginning to dwindle. I had bet Peter a hundred dollars that he would smoke before the ship left Gibraltar. Knowing Peter, that seemed like money for old rope but he was adamant he had kicked the habit.

Inevitably such a long journey was going to be an exercise in tolerance, and this was put to the test early in the second week when Clinton got the fishing lines wrapped around the wind generator. They were untangled quickly to silence the irritating squeak but not long afterwards, in a further lapse of concentration, he also managed to throw our large water bucket overboard. Obligingly, Dirman set about making a new one out of a water container. However, when the tin opener mysteriously disappeared over the side too, those on mother watch spent their time trying to prize open tin cans with the kitchen knife. As we began to use up our supplies of fresh food it was a skill each of us needed to learn quickly.

Fortunately everyone seemed to cope with the mental challenges exceptionally well and, as we discovered, even the wet weather could have unexpected benefits. During one night watch a heavy squall gave way to the most beautiful midnight rainbow, its colours reflecting off the moonlight. It is a rare and exceptional sight and one few of the crew had seen before. In the day the sea life could still be relied upon to break the monotony and there was great excitement one morning when Dirman spotted something in the water. A huge dark grey shape, at least six metres long, appeared on our starboard side. There were splashes of yellow spots along its back and an entourage of pilot fish surrounded its large flat head. It was our first encounter with a whale shark and it wasn't hard to see why the first sailors came back with vivid stories of sea monsters. Fascinated by our presence, it came alongside very slowly and touched our starboard rudder before circling the ship several times. While Aziz grabbed his camera Peter decided it was far too good an opportunity to miss and dived into the sea for a better view. The shark continued to swim with us for the best part of an hour. Finally, perhaps disappointed with the lack of response, it rubbed itself on our port rudder before swimming underneath the ship. Slightly alarmed that the creature's amorous exploits with its new wooden friend were about to damage the hull, I turned on the generator. This seemed to cause the end of its curiosity and it disappeared into the deep again.

Although life had taken on a slower pace and there was more time to relax, there was never a moment for complacency. Conditions in the middle of the ocean could change in an instant. After one quiet night watch the morning light gave shape to a large storm cloud, which had been lingering menacingly for hours, and soon it engulfed us. The heavens opened and the winds whipped up so rapidly that within minutes the ship was being propelled along at six knots. Aziz was having trouble controlling the ship and Daniel rushed to join him at the helm, but both struggled to hold her as thirty-five knots of wind gusted behind us. To slow *Phoenicia* down we had to furl the sail so I sent out a call for all hands on deck.

Shortly afterwards Peter's voice boomed back out of the darkness, 'Does that mean me?'

'Yes it bloody does,' I replied.

By the time everyone was up on deck the waves and wind were battering the ship with alarming force. The gusts whipped the rain into our faces making it difficult to see. Aziz called for everyone to don a life jacket, but most ignored him as we battled to get the ship back under control. Sulhan was shouting at Daniel, Clinton and Peter, who were so intent on pulling on the brailing lines they had forgotten to release the sheet first. Once done, a concerted effort raised the sail to less than a metre below the yard. Our speed through the water fell away, we slowed down to two knots and the danger subsided. The deluge had overwhelmed the bilges and it took twenty minutes of muscle power to pump them out before the extra hands could return to their bunks, leaving the four of us to continue our watch.

With rapidly changing weather conditions it was no surprise that the ship was in need of continual attention and running repairs. Damaged rigging, a split sail, and the more serious problem of a frayed forestay, had to be attended to and fixed. With so much weight hanging above our heads I was concerned about the strength of the upper part of the mast, so we lowered the yard height slightly to where the mast was stronger. Dirman worked on the generator, which had been leaking again, and once he had dealt with this he turned his attention to the electric bilge pump. He took it apart but when reassembled it still stubbornly refused to work, and with the solution remaining elusive he went to find something else to mend. Any questions over whether he could fix a repair were met with the same response – a broad smile and the word *mungkin* meaning maybe. This could mean maybe yes or maybe no, he would not be drawn any further.

Finally, after twenty-four days at sea and a week later than expected, we passed through the doldrums. The rainy squalls abated and we began to pick up the strong northeast winds coming from the West African coast. With them came huge Atlantic rollers of a size and force we had not encountered before. Occasionally a six-metre wave would break across the deck or slam into the beam of the ship and *Phoenicia* would rock and swerve violently, but somehow she managed to stay together and ride it out. For days we continued in this way and although it was exhilarating sailing in these conditions, the constant rocking motion was tiring and the wave pattern was frustrating our attempts to move forward. As we grappled with the elements we were using all available spare time for sleeping.

One morning, as dawn broke, we could see yet another split in the sail below a recent patching. Hours were spent preparing for the yard and sail to come down but by the afternoon, when the winds had not moderated as I had hoped, we were forced to carry out the repairs. Many of the crew had already experienced this procedure when we had rounded the Cape and as soon as the mainsail came down we quickly hoisted the green storm sail. Speed was of the essence; we knew this was no place for a ship to be broached by the powerful white-crested rollers that were surging across our starboard side. Thirty minutes later the repair had been completed and we could hoist the mainsail again.

By now we had notched up a month at sea and were still heading west towards the Americas. Until we could find the winds to push us in the direction of the Azores all we could do was wait and have patience and faith in nature.

~

Water, water, everywhere
And all the boards did shrink
Water, water, everywhere
Nor any drop to drink

Samuel Taylor Coleridge
The Rhyme of the Ancient Mariner

Aziz had stopped speaking to me. For the second time during the expedition the water situation had caused a rift between us. Earlier I had put him in charge of monitoring our supplies and he had been scrupulously checking the number of jerry cans we had got through. However, after an audit of our provisions a month into the journey I reviewed our consumption. In light of the fact that our voyage looked set to continue for another six to seven weeks I realised we could run out of water days before making landfall. We needed to start rationing again and all but essential use had to stop.

Aziz had resumed washing with drinking water five times a day before prayers and he saw the situation in very different terms. His religious beliefs kept him secure in the knowledge that everything would work out as Allah intended and if we died of thirst that was Allah's will. The rest of us felt that perhaps He would like us to use our initiative before we got to that stage. We discussed the possibilities and decided the entire crew should be limited to twenty litres per day. This sparked a heated debate. Aziz tried to persuade me I was exaggerating the seriousness of the situation, but only I was aware of how much longer it was likely to take and no amount of reasoning, entreating or pleading was going to change my mind; in the end he conceded defeat.

The results of our new regime were impressive and our water consumption halved. If we were becalmed in the middle of the ocean I hoped we could last another sixty days. Despite this Aziz remained unmoved and his silent protest continued; he would comply with any requests but wouldn't utter a word in response. It took another three weeks before he would converse with me fully again.

Later, as our long journey to the Azores continued, we changed our water regime for a second time when we discovered that some were drinking far more than others. Peter, in particular, was consuming large amounts of water and not everyone was getting their fair share. In his laid-back way Daniel suggested, if everyone was in agreement, that each person should have their own two-litre bottle per day. Aziz became much happier after this as he could use his personal supply in any way he wished.

We are sons of Canaan from Sidon, the city of the king. Commerce has cast us on this distant shore … in the nineteenth year of Hiram, our mighty king. We embarked from Ezion-geber [Israel] in the Red Sea and voyaged with ten ships. We were at sea together for two years around the land belonging to Ham [Africa] but we were separated by a storm and were no longer with our companions. So we have come here, twelve men and three women on a shore, which I, the Admiral, control. But auspiciously may the exalted gods and goddesses favour us.[1]

Inscription in Phoenician script allegedly found chiselled on a stone near Joao Pessoa, northern Brazil, 1872

By heading so far west we found we were fuelling another debate: had the Phoenicians reached the Americas two thousand years before Christopher Columbus? Although many experts consider the above inscription to be a forgery our Atlantic voyage was giving credence to the possibility that they had made it that far. I knew that before we could hope to turn towards the Azores we would have to journey a long way into the Atlantic, with the pattern of winds and currents in this region it was inevitable. By this point the winds had taken us to within four hundred miles of the coast of South America.

Our foray so far from Africa may have been igniting debate among historians but it was causing great concern for the parents of some younger crew members. They watched our tracker position with increasing alarm, and relatively minor but frustrating technical glitches only worsened their anxieties. There were days when the tracker system would fail or we were unable to send blogs and, although this was bound to happen at times, it did nothing to reassure those eager for news. When Steph had not been mentioned in the blogs for a couple of weeks her mother began to worry and she made an anxious call to the office. Alice reassured her everything was fine and if there were any problems concerning her daughter she would be contacted immediately. Meanwhile Steph was one of the calmest people on board and took our Atlantic marathon in her stride.

Other parents were not as easily placated. One morning an email came through for Daniel, to which Alice had attached a note urging me to read it first. After a quick glance I realised why, as it contained an alarming piece of advice. Daniel's mother was so concerned about the expedition she had sought the opinion of a family friend, a professional skipper who had crossed the Atlantic eight times. The email was a summary of his views and it certainly wasn't pleasant for me to read. He believed we had not understood the nature of the winds in the Atlantic or the purpose of Phoenician boats. According to him they had only ever been used as coastal craft and the only safe way to sail the ocean was in a steel boat under engine power. While acknowledging that the project was an adventure he was convinced that Daniel was in danger and, as he seemed to think we would put into a port soon, he advised him to jump ship at the next possible opportunity.

The email was a shock, and although I had heard his arguments many times before it made me question my convictions. I briefly wondered if the risks I was taking were too great and whether this leg was doomed to fail. It was a voyage of discovery and in testing the boundaries of current thinking and our knowledge of ancient seafarers we had had to make some assumptions: about the Phoenicians' circumnavigation of Africa, their understanding of the winds and currents, and the route they took. Of course there were risks but I believed that I had weighed up the dangers as carefully as I could before embarking on the venture. I had been involved in every aspect of *Phoenicia*'s design and construction, and throughout this process I had been mindful of her suitability for ocean-going conditions. I mulled over his arguments.

Phoenicia had been based on an ocean-going merchant galley, not on the small coastal craft they had used to navigate rivers and harbours, and she was certainly proving to be seaworthy. To sail a square-rigged vessel up the coast of West Africa beyond the equator would have been difficult, if not impossible, to achieve by hugging the coast. For most of the year the current would have flowed from the north against their passage, and even with oarsmen they would have found it difficult to row a fifty-tonne ship against the strong currents and headwinds they would have encountered. Given that they had not chosen to battle their way up the coast they would have had to sail out into the mid Atlantic. Why struggle against the elements when following the prevailing winds and currents would have been the easiest route? The Phoenicians were the first seafarers who had learnt to navigate by the stars and with this information they had no need to stay within sight of land.

Having given the matter serious thought I deleted the email and sent a note to Alice instructing her to tell anyone who asked that we had never received it. Although I knew Daniel was calm and sensible the message had made me analyse my convictions, and I was aware of the potentially devastating effect it could have on crew morale during the most challenging part of our longest leg. A few days later Daniel's girlfriend contacted the office. Having discovered what had happened she wanted to apologise for any distress caused and asked Alice to ignore the email.

After five weeks sailing, *Phoenicia* was finally on the same page of the chart as the Azores, but we were still heading in the direction of the Windward Islands. It was a relief when we began to pick up some speed and while most of us concentrated on preparing the mainsail for hoisting, Peter and Clinton were jumping up and down with excitement, distracted by the presence of a small shark. It was a terrific sight to see the purple and white stripes of the Phoenician empire flying over the Atlantic. The brilliant sunshine caught the crest of the waves and *Phoenicia*'s sail billowed out, enabling her bow to push through the water. With the sail change our speed increased to four knots. It was nearly the end of May and now, on a clear night, we could make out the Pole Star, just below the Plough. The Phoenicians were the first to understand the significance of this star for navigation and would have relied on it to find true north and to determine their latitude.

By this stage the Caribbean was so close we could have reached it in a few days, not that I was intending on having a tropical island break. Despite the fact that we had already consumed half our drinking water supplies I knew with rationing we would have enough until we reached the Azores, but the jerry cans were serving another purpose: as well as keeping us alive the water had been maintaining our ballast levels. I was concerned that we might be getting too light so I decided to fill the empty cans with seawater using the diesel bilge pump that sat on deck. Some of the crew got to work bringing up the cans while Clinton placed one end of the bilge pump hose over the side into the sea, leaving the other end on the deck for Peter to connect to the pump. Not realising part of the hose was already in the water, and briefly distracted, Peter didn't immediately pick it up. Seconds later I turned to see the hose slithering rapidly across the deck and before I could take action it had dropped silently over the side. Clinton volunteered to dive in after it but we were travelling at three knots and losing a vital piece of hose was bad enough but losing a member of crew was unthinkable. However, without the hose we had no bilge pump, and without this pump assisting the other the hull would soon fill with water. We would only be able to last two or three days before the bilges were overwhelmed and I wasn't sure we could even make it to the Caribbean in time.

Dirman looked at me in bewilderment. He didn't need a strong command of English to express what he was thinking. 'How the hell did you let that happen?' was etched into the quizzical look on his face. I was so embarrassed I couldn't bring myself to ask him to help find a solution. Instead Peter and I disappeared below to work out a plan and eventually we found a smaller tube, which we taped tightly to the pump. To my great relief it seemed to work, but with a much shorter tube the pump could no longer stay on deck and it had to be taken below to sit next to the bilge hatch. We spent twenty minutes rigging up the new system. A silencer dampened the noise and we tried to draw as many of the fumes out of the ship as we could but inevitably some seeped back into the cabin. It was far from ideal but at least we could continue our voyage.

Not long after this our progress slowed dramatically. The wind vanished, the sea was smooth and flat and the mainsail hung limply from the yard. Again we would have to wait while the elements tested our patience. We spent the days watching shearwaters skimming the ocean and large shoals of tuna darting and weaving through the water. At least a hundred had accompanied us from the equator and there was always one seemingly prepared to sacrifice itself on the hook. However, the best entertainment would come when the flying fish became airborne; then the hunted became the hunters and we would gather to watch the chase. Like torpedoes, the tuna would fix on their target while the gulls pursued from above. As the fish hit the water a frenzy of splashing would follow as tuna and gull competed to catch it. If the birds won the contest they would fight each other for the spoils amidst a cacophony of shrieking and squawking. The victor would hurry away with its catch and the process would begin again.

The rest of the time the crew kept boredom at bay by using the deck as a gym and the sea as their swimming pool. Any unread books were devoured, regardless of their subject matter, and the few magazines on board had been picked through from cover to cover several times. When not reading we would delve into a new topic of conversation, mull over the political ramifications of the recent British election or ponder how each country would fare in the football World Cup. If any of these failed to ignite our enthusiasm there was always our endless obsession with food and recipes to fall back on.

> *Hello my baby*
> *Hello my honey*
> *Hello my ragtime gal,*
> *Send me a kiss by wire*
> *Baby my heart's on fire*
> *And if you refuse me*
> *Then you'll lose me*
> *And you'll be left alone*
> *So baby, telephone and tell me* ... makan pagi!
> (Indonesian for breakfast)

As he burst into song, Daniel's words broke through the silence and floated down to the sleeping crew below. It was the most original call to breakfast so far. Laid out on the galley table were bread, jams, tinned fruit and his speciality, home-made granola.

With much time on our hands meals were an important part of the day. They signalled the watch changes, kept the monotony at bay and lifted our spirits, although that could depend on who was cooking. Creativity in the kitchen allowed different personalities to express themselves, and with each member having to cook at least once or twice every four days everyone developed their own signature dishes.

For the Indonesians, fish and rice formed their staple diet but each had his own distinctive style. Dirman loved deep-frying fish in flour and spices. He called his fried fillets of tuna *ayam laut*, meaning chicken of the sea, and after weeks on board they did begin to taste remarkably like chicken. Sulhan had a penchant for making fish head soup and sometimes the aroma would waft through the boards, reaching those on night watch as he heated it up for a midnight snack. Aziz made liberal use of every hot spice he could lay his hands on, and had become a master at disguising the tasteless corned beef that we occasionally tried to sneak into our dishes.

By now Steph had mastered the art of pizza making and while she still produced cakes and biscuits, this was usually after some heavy hinting from the rest of the crew. Clinton was a fan of bread baking and Daniel was a creative chef, throwing whatever came to hand into the pan and coming up with a great taste every time. Peter was less sure of himself in the kitchen, but he found a niche making corn fritters for breakfast and a range of fish curries for lunch or supper. After several weeks he had found a formula that seemed to work and served with rice it usually turned out well. However, Peter's love of talking and asking questions were about to get him into trouble and it came to a head over food. Asking Clinton's opinion of every meal he produced was becoming a habit and Clinton was growing increasingly irritated by the interrogation. One evening, as we tucked into his latest offering, Peter turned to Clinton to ask him what he thought. Clinton clenched his jaw tightly and pushed the food around his plate.

'It tastes like fish with a can of tomatoes on top,' he growled.

The rest of us sat in silence. Clinton, who rarely filtered what he said, had bluntly but accurately summed up the meal. I warned Peter not to persist in antagonising him but a few days later Clinton snapped.

'He wants to kill me!' Peter blurted out, visibly shaken by the exchange. 'He said, "If you question me about your cooking again I'll murder you",' he explained.

Clinton was a tall and imposing figure, making him an intimidating opponent and Peter was convinced he might carry out his threat. I doubted that I would come on deck one morning to find

Peter hanging from one of the brailing lines, but I didn't want the situation escalating any further. I told the two of them to sort out their differences or take separate watches. They agreed that Clinton would switch to the other watch, but I warned them that if tensions arose again one of them would have to leave at the next port.

Fortunately repairs provided some distraction. Four holes in the mainsail had been getting larger over the previous days and needed attention. To save us the effort of lowering a tonne of yard and sail onto the deck we decided to patch them on the move. This was a labour-intensive operation and, while Clinton stitched from the windward side of the sail, Dirman and Daniel took it in turns to sit on the guardrail on the leeward side. If the wind blew too strongly there was a danger the sail would push them off the rail and into the water so Steph, Peter and I held the sail tightly with the help of an attached rope. Once Clinton had pushed the needle back through the canvas, instructions were given to the leeward sewer as to where to feed the needle in for the return stitch. This involved a considerable amount of trial and error, with shouts of 'up a bit … more to the heavens … no lower … no back'. Each of these instructions had to be translated for Dirman and the exercise doubled up as a beginner's lesson in Indonesian. It was difficult to tell how much English Dirman had learnt from the experience but he found the entire process highly amusing. After an hour and a half four postcard-sized patches had been sewn in place.

Finally on 12th June, after fifty-two days at sea, we began to turn east; *Phoenicia* was heading towards the Azores at last. To mark the occasion we had a small celebration, but we knew we still had over one and a half thousand miles to go and sailing was slow. We were on the edge of a high-pressure system, the barometer was rising and there wasn't a cloud in sight. With calm seas, deep blue rolling waves and only light winds we meandered along at just over two knots. We continued to pray for a bit of a 'whoosh', an expression that had become rather popular over the previous weeks. I knew the stronger clockwise rotating winds generated from the Azores high were ahead, but it was taking a long time for us to get far enough north to take advantage of them.

Aziz had continued to collect rainwater during every downpour to supplement our supplies. He joked that if we got down to twenty cans we should hijack a ship and demand water – at least I assumed he was joking. As we got nearer to the Azores I hoped I could ease up on our restrictions but until then rationing stayed in place.

By this stage we had been encountering more traffic: a large warship had overtaken us a few days earlier and now we caught the attention of a passing yacht. *Sophia* came in for a closer look, her skipper intrigued to come across such an unusual-looking vessel. Carl and Rachel had recently left Bermuda and were heading to Norway via the Azores, but they would reach land a long time before *Phoenicia*. They enquired if there was something we needed, but pride and reserve prevented us from asking for any of the items we had finished. However, we must have looked in a sorry state as a few minutes later they were alongside throwing us a bag containing popcorn, olive oil, cookies and sachets of Italian roast coffee. It was an extremely kind gesture and their timing was perfect, as not long before we had used up our last drop of cooking oil. We returned the favour by giving them a bottle of Delheim's best rosé wine. We waved goodbye and within a couple of hours *Sophia* was out of sight. *Phoenicia* was alone again.

It was the end of June and although we continued to make some progress towards the east the Azores high appeared to keep moving northwards, remaining just out of reach. To console ourselves we celebrated seventy continuous days at sea by eating our new supply of cookies and popcorn. As *Phoenicia* drifted along we began to spot more debris in the waters around us. Clinton would dive in to recover any potentially useful items and our tender rapidly began to fill with pink fishing buoys, which I hoped we could sell to the fishermen in Horta. Meanwhile chess mania had broken out on board with almost endless games being played back to back. The Indonesians were winning convincingly so every small victory over them was celebrated, even though they gave us many chances. A raised eyebrow would indicate 'Are you sure?' but once you had committed to a move they would go in for the kill. It was a great deal of fun in rather frustrating circumstances. By this stage we were less than five hundred miles from Flores, the most westerly island in the Azores, and just over six hundred miles from Faial, our intended destination.

On 7th July our circumstances began to change and as the winds freshened our speed increased to six knots for the first time in many weeks. Our loyal shoal of tuna had no difficulty keeping up with us and, as if anticipating the excitement of land, the wildlife took on a new burst of energy. Having been largely absent for three weeks, the shearwaters returned in large numbers. Now bonito appeared and joined forces with the tuna to hunt down vast shoals of sardines, the frenzied splashing creating a considerable noise as these predatory groups passed by. Later in the day we encountered a much bigger fish. As we surfed over a large wave *Phoenicia* rolled to one side and, as we rolled back, a young sperm whale suddenly appeared beside us less than a boat length away. Shocked by our presence it began to thrash around violently in the water before diving astern, its tail disappearing into the white froth it had created. We had heard nothing knock against the ship and its back looked fine but perhaps the barnacles on our keel had caught its tail. Our encounter and the prospect of landfall created a buzz of excitement on board.

Although our intended port of call was Horta, on the island of Faial, our route was going to take us to within forty miles of Flores. Our passage from Ascension had been far longer than any of us had anticipated and we decided we should make landfall there first. Finally, after eighty-four days at sea our feet touched solid earth again.

The Azores Question

Were the Portuguese the first to find the Azores in the 1420s? Historians have fiercely debated this question for centuries. Stories of islands in far-flung regions of the Atlantic go back to the ancient Greeks and Romans, but what evidence is there to link ancient mariners with this particular archipelago? Do an equestrian statue and a cache of gold and copper coins point to a much earlier discovery?

The mystery centres around one particular island, the smallest and one of the most westerly in the Azores named Corvo. In 1567, Damien de Goes, a writer and chronicler of the Portuguese kingdom, wrote an account of an intriguing story he claimed had come from the first Portuguese explorers. When they arrived on the island they were said to have found a statue of a man seated on a horse, on a rock towering above them. His right arm was outstretched and one finger was pointing west to the ocean beyond. On the base of the statue was an inscription, almost worn away and in a language they did not understand. The image was sketched and taken to King Manuel in Lisbon who, on seeing it, sent a man to the island to remove the carving and bring it to Portugal, but during the process it was broken. Only fragments survived and subsequently these were lost.

The trail goes cold for another two hundred years until an article appeared in an academic journal in Sweden in 1778. Johan Frans Podolyn, a Swedish numismatist, wrote about a discovery allegedly made thirty years earlier on Corvo. After days of rough seas and heavy rains a clay pot emerged from the ruins of a stone building. Inside were a large number of gold and copper coins. Some were sent to Lisbon and nine forwarded to a renowned Spanish historian and numismatist, Father Henrique Florez. Later he gave them to Podolyn. What made these coins interesting was their origin and date: two were from Cyrene, an ancient Greek colony, in what is modern-day Libya, and seven others, two gold and five copper, were Punic coins. Every one of them was dated to the 4th century BC. Had these coins been left by the Phoenicians, or another ancient civilisation, nearly two thousand years before the Portuguese had arrived? If ancient seafarers had got this far how much further had they gone? Was this the reason the stone horseman was pointing west into the Atlantic towards the New World?

The validity of these claims has been debated ever since. The stone statue has been dismissed as a fable or a strangely shaped volcanic rock, while it has been suggested that later settlers brought the coins to Corvo. Even without these stories, should we dismiss their arrival entirely?

The Phoenicians were not afraid to venture beyond the Mediterranean and had many colonies along the Atlantic coast, both in Europe and North Africa. They may have found the Azores by accident, having been blown off course when rounding the African coast. Perhaps by following the prevailing winds and currents they had come upon the islands and realised they made a perfect staging post for re-entering the Mediterranean. Of course, they could have left the safety of the coast intentionally and, in their hunger for trade and expansion, sailed out into the Atlantic actively searching for new lands. Their trade routes had made them rich and powerful and they guarded them from their rivals under a veil of secrecy. They perpetuated a myth that it was a dangerous folly to go beyond the Straits of Gibraltar, even though they ventured out into these waters regularly.[2] If the Phoenicians had knowledge of these islands they would have set out on their circumnavigation of Africa confident of their north Atlantic route home. My journey was convincing me they had discovered the Azores, but many Portuguese historians are so reluctant to consider the possibility of any pre-Christian contact with the islands that the subject is almost taboo. Until more evidence is found the proof remains elusive.

21

We had a difficult mooring on the edge of the harbour in Flores and *Phoenicia* was subjected to the rough Atlantic swell, but we were able to carry out essential repairs. Our visit had coincided with an annual cultural festival and the crew, hungry for some outside stimulation, made the most of what was on offer. Locals showed us around so we could see the lush green hillsides covered in the flowers that give the island its name. The volcanic activity that created it has left strange geological formations: huge columns of rock point to the sky and seven large craters have filled with water to form deep blue lakes.

Despite taking an unscheduled stop on this tiny and remote island we managed to pick up a new crew member. Randy Getty was a sign-writer from New Mexico and, in a bizarre co-incidence, he had applied to join *Phoenicia* nearly two years before but had never managed to make it on board. He had been helping crew a yacht across the Atlantic and a week after he arrived in Flores he was amazed to see *Phoenicia* sail into the harbour. As I had already seen his application I was happy to welcome him on board. One of his passions was black and white photography and he wasted no time shooting roll after roll of film. Due to work commitments his journey with us was limited to the short trip to the island of Faial, but he had finally been granted his wish to sail on board *Phoenicia*.

After a few days in Flores we sailed the small distance to Horta. We came in past the breakwater covered in paintings left by visiting sailors, and into the harbour surrounded by a cluster of whitewashed houses. We remained there for twelve days while we restocked with plenty of fresh fruit, vegetables, eggs and meat. We also took the opportunity to paint purple and white stripes on our reserve sail to match the mainsail. By the time we left we had a compliment of ten on board. Yuri and Niklas rejoined the ship and Edward Sadler arrived from England. At nineteen he was the youngest crew member to have taken part. Reluctantly, Peter decided it was time to leave. Although he remained full of enthusiasm for the trip, Vanessa was missing him desperately and had sent several emails asking him to return to South Africa. We knew it was going to be much quieter without him, but he promised to keep in touch and as a parting gift he left us his beloved fishing rods.

Randy Getty flew back to the US but not before painting a picture of *Phoenicia* on the quayside. This is a tradition most yachtsmen observe before leaving Horta and being a sign-writer it was natural that Randy should take on the task. When he had finished we gathered round to view the final image. It was hard to know what to say and, for once, the crew were speechless as we studied the representation of the ship that lay in front of us. It was plain to see that Randy had painted it while under the influence of one or two bottles of liquid refreshment. After he had left a couple of crew spent a number of hours and used several litres of paint producing a more realistic representation.

My plan on leaving Horta was to sail north, pick up the edge of the Azores High and catch a lift on the winds and currents that would push us around to the east. Only after travelling north then east would we be able to start our passage down the Portuguese coast towards Gibraltar. This would take several days and would appear to those tracking our progress that we were heading towards the UK, but in mid August it seemed the only viable way to get where we wanted in our square-rigged vessel.

As we began to head north the conditions were calm and the winds light. Occasionally a rain cloud passed by, briefly soaking the deck. For three days the fishing lines remained stashed away. Although we were missing Peter's expertise and passion for angling, this was largely due to the fact that we had seen little sign of any fish. Then, as if *Phoenicia* had summoned them to her side, a large shoal of tuna joined us again. Daniel grabbed Peter's fishing rod, jumped into action and twenty minutes later three fish lay on the deck. Steph promptly gathered them up and disappeared into the galley. We were delighted our fortunes had changed because everyone knew the alternative was corned beef. It had been such an unpopular choice we still had forty tins left almost two years after leaving Syria.

By the fourth day the night's rain and wind shifts had given way to blue skies and warm sunshine and we took the opportunity to relax. The excitement caused by the appearance of two large whales lifted the afternoon's lethargy. There was a scramble for cameras followed by an awed silence as they swam past, one behind the other, blowing water spouts into the air as they went. Later, as the day's light faded, a pod of dolphins came to within metres of the ship. They seemed to be focused on hunting but still had time for some impressive feats of acrobatics, shooting into the air and belly flopping into the sea as they made their way past us. It was hard not to feel a sense of joy every time they made an appearance, and unsurprising that for centuries mariners had believed their presence heralded good luck.

The following day the winds gathered strength and we began cutting through the water at nearly seven knots. This was touching the top range of our safe speed but I needed to get *Phoenicia* as far east as I could before the winds changed direction. The skies clouded over and it began to rain, which made everything not wrapped in plastic sodden, both above and below deck. The waves gathered height, white foam curling over their peaks, and time on the helm became more uncomfortable as *Phoenicia* bounced around in the swell. To cheer us up Yuri cooked pancakes for breakfast while Clinton got to work preparing a batch of doughnuts. Steph turned her cooking skills to making cakes, although these morale-boosting treats were no help to Aziz as Ramadan had started.

Over the following days the wind changed direction many

times, pushing us south, north and finally towards the east. It was frustrating but I was not unduly concerned. I knew, given time, the northerly and westerly winds would come as they had always done in this part of the Atlantic. While we waited for more favourable winds we filled our days with games of chess and cards. It was a revelation to discover Dirman was as good at cards as he was at chess, and everyone he played he beat decisively.

The weather began to close in, and as the days became misty and cold we were forced to don more and more layers of clothes in an effort to keep warm while at the helm. No longer sporting his trademark shorts, Sulhan had taken to wearing a fleece, gloves, and a scarf neatly wrapped around his head. This earned him the honour of best-dressed member of the team. Visibility was poor and, in spite of keeping a two-hourly radar check, one ship managed to get within a couple of miles of us before it was spotted emerging out of the gloom. We had reached a speed of five knots while the other ship was travelling at fourteen, so we were closing in on each other more quickly than I would have liked. Fortunately they must have picked us up on their radar as we passed each other with just under five hundred metres to spare. It was a comfortable distance but a rather unpleasant surprise.

By the third week of August we were making good progress towards the Portuguese coast, despite being closer to the UK than to the Mediterranean. It was the rotational nature of the winds and currents dictating our route that would have allowed the Phoenicians to reach what they called the Cassiterides or Tin Islands, probably the Scilly Isles and Cornwall. Here they would have bartered for both tin and lead with the Cornish inhabitants who were 'clad in black cloaks and tunics reaching to their feet [and] bearded like goats'.[1] I admired their bravery in crossing the Bay of Biscay and sailing along the coast of Cornwall. These were formidable waters to venture into in a ship that needed to sail downwind.

As we came within fifty miles of the coast of Lisbon we encountered the first of two traffic separation zones. We were entering one of the busiest shipping regions in the world and we found ourselves dwarfed by huge container ships and tankers. This was a modern peril a Phoenician ship would never have had to encounter. Alarmingly, strong winds kept pushing us towards the path of oncoming traffic so we had to reverse and heave-to north of the zone. We waited until the winds were more favourable and then we entered the fray again. Before dawn we sighted HMS *Gloucester* heading off on patrol, then some time later the *Grand Princess*, a large cruise liner, loomed above us in the early morning light as she sailed past on her way to Cadiz. On learning our story her captain decided to come a little closer so her passengers could take a look. What they saw was a bedraggled Phoenician crew battling the winds, damp and mist and I wondered how many of them would have wanted to swap places with us.

We had made it through the first zone but we were on a constant lookout for shipping. Sometimes there would be seven or eight vessels within a few miles of us, which made watch duty a busy time, particularly at night. At one point we counted thirty-three ships coming at us from every direction. The second separation zone was as much a test of courage as the first, and to add to the excitement it appeared that a number of ships preferred to bend the rules as much as possible by sailing up the central reservation zone, rather than keeping to their traffic lanes. Once we had rounded Point Sagres we began heading towards Cape Trafalgar and Gibraltar, and by remaining reasonably close to the coast we were able to keep out of the way of shipping to the south of our position. With fifty miles to go to reach Gibraltar, the Spanish coast came into sight and we could make out Morocco's mountainous outline on our starboard side.

The final passage along the Strait of Gibraltar was a nail-biting experience. A sea mist shrouded everything in a thick cloak of grey and strong headwinds threatened to prevent us going any further. The only way we could tackle these winds was to pick up the strong current, forcing us to position *Phoenicia* near the centre of the Strait and face oncoming ships in the adjacent traffic lane. In the end it was a strategy that paid dividends but it was a tense night and we were relieved to make landfall the following morning.

After twenty-seven days at sea we reached Gibraltar. *Phoenicia* took her place alongside the yachts at the Ocean Village Marina, the hosts for our stay. Behind us rose a wall of glass-fronted high-rise buildings. We had been thrown back into the modern world again but around us there were reminders of the history we were reliving. From the marina we could see the rock the Phoenicians had named Calpe or hollow stone and across the strait we could make out the mountains of North Africa. These landmarks were reputed to be the Pillars of Hercules, the gateway from one world to another, from the sea to the vast open ocean. This place had been of great strategic importance to the Phoenicians, the bridge between their Mediterranean and Atlantic trade.

It appeared that the expedition had already attracted press coverage and, along with marina staff, a small crowd and the local media were there to welcome us. During our stay the Director of the Gibraltar Museum, Professor Finlayson, gave us a tour of the museum's Phoenician artefacts. While excavating Gorham's Cave, one of the one hundred and forty caves that form part of the rock, archaeologists had uncovered evidence of Phoenician settlement spanning five centuries. Among the discoveries were thousands of offerings, leading them to conclude that the cave had been used as a temple, most probably dedicated to the Phoenician god Melqart. Melqart was the guardian of the city of Tyre, and the Phoenicians believed that he protected both their sailors and their trade. By building temples to him in the places they colonised they were attempting to ensure their safety and success. It was exciting for us to get a small glimpse into the lives of those we were honouring on our journey and for many of the crew it helped add another dimension to the expedition. For me, a new piece of information was of particular significance. I was told about the discovery of rock paintings in southern Spain dating to 1500 BC depicting ships, very similar to *Phoenicia,* transiting the Strait of Gibraltar. If the dating of these images is correct it would suggest much greater maritime activity in this region far earlier than previously thought. This would make a successful circumnavigation of Africa by 600 BC seem even more plausible.

With a five-day stop some of the crew used the opportunity to relax and explore the cafes, shops and restaurants that lined the quay front, while others took to the local bars to enjoy a good British pint. One of our days was spent sailing *Phoenicia* around the coast with a BBC film crew. They were making a documentary called *Ancient Worlds* and footage of a Phoenician ship under sail was just what they were looking for.

During our stay Daniel left the expedition and returned to the States, but crew continued coming forward to participate. We were joined by Danielle Eubank, the expedition artist, who was hoping to get some inspiration for an exhibition she was holding the following year, and by John Horseman, a British supporter of the project. This took our numbers to eleven and we left Gibraltar in buoyant mood, ready to start the Mediterranean leg of our voyage. We were heading to Tunisia and Carthage, one of the Phoenician's most famous and important cities.

22

Much silver trickled away from the fiery ground and as they melted, the silver bearing ores formed countless rivulets of pure silver. The natives (of Iberia) did not know how to exploit it but once the Phoenicians heard of the affair they bought the silver in exchange for objects of negligible value. The Phoenicians took the silver to Greece, to Asia and to all other countries then known, thus obtaining great riches. It is said that such was the cupidity of the traders that they replaced the lead anchors of their ships with silver ones after there was no more room for silver in the vessels and there was still a great quantity of metal left over. [1]

Diodorus Siculus, 1st century BC

By the 8th century BC the Phoenicians had begun to expand rapidly, creating settlements along the Iberian coast. Combining astute commercial acumen with maritime dominance they wasted no time in exploiting their position, and the silver trade proved to be highly lucrative. Although the chief beneficiary was the city of Tyre, the merchants of Gadir (modern-day Cadiz) also became wealthy and powerful by capitalising on this commerce.

Phoenician merchant fleets would have dominated the Mediterranean at this time, as ships like ours travelled back and forth from their trading posts laden with goods. Battling the winds and seas as we were doing, the Phoenicians set out on their journeys with one purpose in mind: to trade. With a capacity of between one and five hundred tonnes[2] every square inch of their merchant ships would have been filled with goods: food, wine and olive oil in amphorae and the larger four-handled urns, called *pithoi*, pottery with a distinctive red glaze and rolls of silk from the East, which the Phoenicians dyed purple, the colour so highly prized throughout the Mediterranean. On their return the same vessels would have been loaded to the gunnels with silver from Iberia, tin from the Scilly Isles and Cornwall, gold, copper and lead from the Atlas Mountains, as well as animal skins, ivory and salt from the Sahara. This was a well-run commercial machine and the Phoenicians shrewdly exploited every valuable commodity they could.

As we left Gibraltar we followed the easterly setting current that would take us towards Tunis, and we hoisted the storm sail for the strong westerly winds we knew were on their way. For the new members of crew it was a baptism of fire as within forty-eight hours we were in the throes of a force eight gale. The winds were gusting up to forty knots and as the seas became bigger we began to surf over huge waves. Helming became a test of nerve. One minute we would be coasting downwards, dwarfed by an eight-metre wall of water, the next we would rise up to reach the white crests, which foamed and spluttered and sprayed, before being tipped back down again. We had left the main current and were heading across to the Algerian coast. It was a relief that with such strong winds there was little traffic coming either way, as while we were being thrown around in angry seas there was little we could do to radically alter our course.

Despite the discomfort on board, the strong westerly winds allowed us to cover over four hundred miles in four days, more than half the distance to Carthage. We had crossed the Greenwich meridian, been able to switch back to our mainsail and were keeping ten miles off the Algerian coast, where we could take advantage of the easterly current running along the top of North Africa. We remained this distance from the coast despite the increase in traffic. The tankers, container vessels and cruise liners were huge monsters in comparison to our little craft and any one of them could have crushed us without even noticing.

After twenty-nine days of observing Ramadan, Aziz was able to eat during the day again and to celebrate Danielle cooked a feast of lamb with spices, as we joined him in marking the start of Eid. The following day the winds abated and our passage became easier. It was while we were sailing through calmer waters that Yuri spotted a large object gently bobbing on the waves. As we got closer I could see the outline of a jet ski, four panniers sealed with plastic strapped to its sides. There were no signs of life; whoever had been riding it had disappeared. Before I had time to utter a word, curiosity got the better of Clinton and he launched himself off the boat and began swimming towards it. We threw him a knife and he scrambled onto the jet ski before carefully cutting open one of the boxes. Inside he discovered rows of neatly packaged blocks.

'What is it?' Yuri shouted.

Clinton held one above his head, 'Hashish,' he called back.

We had unwittingly stumbled on a smuggling operation that had gone badly wrong. Each pannier must have weighed ten kilograms and after making a quick calculation Niklas' eyes widened with amazement.

'That's at least sixty thousand dollars worth,' he announced.

For a few seconds we contemplated the value of what was floating in front of us, and then I gave Clinton the order to cut the bags from the jet ski and we watched as they sank out of sight.

I had no desire to find out if anyone was coming back for the goods so we immediately sailed on, but I began to wonder if I had been too hasty. I had left a valuable jet ski behind and in international waters it was mine to take. Ten minutes later we returned, roped the jet ski to *Phoenicia*, and towed it behind us. Later we hauled it on board and discovered a rope was caught in its turbine and there was no petrol in the tank. We found a number of documents stashed inside the glove compartment: one showed the jet ski had been bought by a Spanish woman three weeks earlier for ten thousand euros, while others gave coordinates marking a point just a few miles off the coast of Marbella. It must have been blown a long way off course by the time we found it. Aziz wanted to head to the Spanish coast to report the incident but I knew *Phoenicia* could be held by the police for weeks as part of an investigation. Instead I asked Alice to report the incident to the British police so they could contact the Spanish authorities. The jet ski remained on deck, covered with canvas, until we returned to Syria.

Over the next few days we began to close in on the port of Sidi Bou Said in Tunisia, ahead of our expected arrival date. In the final twenty-four hours *Phoenicia* hit strong winds and rough seas again. We entered the Bay of Carthage at a staggering speed of seven knots and I wondered if we would be able to slow down enough to make a safe landfall. Eventually, as the light faded, we managed to anchor in the choppy waters outside the harbour, relieved to have arrived and looking forward to exploring Carthage.

23

The small harbour of Sidi Bou Said was full so we spent our entire stay anchored just outside its walls. It was not an ideal mooring, and as the seas remained rough we were forced to put out two anchors to hold our position. Danielle returned to the States with notebooks full of sketches and paintings and John made his way back to the UK. The rest of us were keen to do some exploring. This was the nearest port of entry to Carthage and we wanted to see the remains of the ancient city.

The establishment of a settlement at Carthage is steeped in myth and legend. According to some ancient sources its founder and first queen was Dido, the sister of the King of Tyre. It is beyond dispute that the Tyrians founded a colony there and gave it the name Carthage, meaning New City, and it wasn't long before the new inhabitants began exchanging cloth, pottery and jewellery for gold, silver, tin and other metals found along the Mediterranean and African coasts. They were so successful that Carthage flourished and became one of the largest cities in the ancient world. From here they founded many other colonies and over the centuries it came to wield great religious, political and commercial power. It was no wonder the Romans felt so threatened by their success that they levelled it to the ground in 146 BC. With this brutal act of destruction most traces of its existence disappeared into the dust, but hints of a great Phoenician stronghold still remain.

The remnants of the two ports are some of the best-preserved and most significant parts of their city. The Romans, realising their value, repaired and preserved them to use as the collection point for all their African produce. They lie adjacent to each other and from above the outline resembles a keyhole, with an oblong lagoon serving as the commercial port, beyond which lay a circular inner harbour with an island at its centre. This was the military port and could only be accessed through the basin of the commercial one. What is known of the scale of activities here came from the writings of Polybius, who was based at Carthage when it was destroyed.[1] He created a picture of life at the time of the Phoenicians, describing a busy port where merchant vessels and warships would come and go through an opening seventy-feet wide, which was closed behind them with iron chains. The warships or triremes made their way into the inner harbour where over two hundred other warships would have been moored. Here the admiral of the port watched over them and controlled this traffic from the central island.

Merchant vessels like *Phoenicia* would have remained in the outer harbour and there would have been many of them there; the Egyptian envoy to Tyre, Wen-Amon, tells of fleets of up to fifty Phoenician ships.[2] It must have been a colourful and noisy scene with workers loading and unloading heavy cargo, merchants checking their precious goods and sailors preparing each vessel for its next voyage. It was an image that helped to bring one more piece of *Phoenicia*'s fascinating history to life.

After one afternoon spent wandering around the ruins a few of the crew went to browse the shops lining the entrance to the site. Yuri had stopped at a stall to look at the souvenirs when there was a sudden commotion behind him. A woman began screaming and as Yuri turned to see what had happened he glimpsed Clinton's long legs sprinting across the car park. It soon became clear that the woman was a shopkeeper. As a stream of angry words spilled from her mouth she pointed to an empty cage on the ground then waved her arms in Clinton's direction. Yuri recalled seeing something inside the pen a few minutes earlier and the sequence of events started to fall into place. He tried to calm the woman before dashing off after him.

By this time Clinton was kneeling on the ground in animated

conversation with the creature he had released from confinement. In front of him was a tortoise, its legs and head retracted into the safety of its shell.

'Go, go, go,' Clinton insisted. 'Run, you're free now.'

Yuri watched in amazement. 'What are you doing?' he asked.

'I'm setting it free,' Clinton replied as if this was a perfectly normal thing to do.

Yuri was lost for words. He looked down at the bemused reptile, which was still doing a remarkably good impression of a rock, and wondered if he should explain to Clinton the obvious flaw in his master plan. Instead he decided to take the direct approach.

'It's not a wild animal it's a pet and you've just stolen it. You've got to return it to the woman before she calls the police,' Yuri urged him.

By now the shopkeeper's screams had attracted an uncomfortable amount of attention. Clinton thought about it for a minute, reluctantly picked up his new friend, and slowly carried it back to the woman. She grabbed it before beginning another angry tirade, at which point they beat a hasty retreat back to the ship. It was time to leave Tunisia before someone got arrested.

With final preparations done we put our backs into hauling up the anchors only to find we had acquired another one, along with a tangled mess of nets and two terracotta pots. A fisherman's anchor must have become entangled in our own and inside one of the pots was his catch staring back at us, its tentacles spilling from its watery prison. It would be octopus on the menu that evening, although it turned out to be a rather chewy supper.

As we made our exit *Phoenicia* was buffeted by strong northwesterly winds. We had two small islands and a headland to clear and it took nearly twelve hours before we were free from danger. After this we hoisted the mainsail for the relatively short journey of a hundred and thirty miles to Malta. On board three new British crew – Natalie Lumby, Robert Onion and Colin Moore

– had settled in well, helming, pumping the bilges and generally helping out where needed. We made steady progress, and despite light winds and overcast skies a helpful nudge from a southeasterly setting current kept us moving along. After eighty miles we passed the island of Pantelleria, once famous for its construction of Punic warships, and from there it was a relatively short and uneventful hop to Malta. On 22nd September, after four days at sea, we made landfall.

We sailed past the solid pale stone ramparts that surrounded the entrance to Manoel Island. The harbour lies in a sheltered position, held within the protective arms of two peninsulas and linked to the mainland by a small bridge. Once we had reached the marina we took our place among a collection of yachts and super yachts lined up in increasing size, their sleek lines gleaming in the sunshine.

The fortress that stands on Manoel Island was built by one of the Grandmasters of the Knights of Malta, Christian crusaders who ruled for two hundred and sixty-eight years. The Holy Roman Emperor, Charles V, gave them the island in 1530 in return for an annual gift of a Maltese falcon, which represented the military might of his empire.[1] Much later it became a British Protectorate and during the 1940s the British Naval supply base there was referred to as HMS *Phoenicia*.[2]

The Phoenicians probably settled on the island early in their colonisation of the Mediterranean, and at the end of the 17th century the Knights of Malta uncovered two marble slabs bearing inscriptions to the Phoenician god Melqart. They were written in both Phoenician and Greek, allowing scholars to unlock the meaning of the Phoenician script, the forerunner to many modern alphabets.[3] However, the legacy of Phoenician occupation goes far beyond this archaeological discovery: a genetic study has revealed that a proportion of the Maltese population alive today are descended from Phoenician ancestors, while the language itself may have had Punic origins.[4] Although Malta did not come close to the size, wealth or power of Carthage it would have been a significant outpost in such an important strategic location. Positioned in the centre of the Mediterranean and with the advantage of a protected harbour they named the island

Malat, meaning refuge.

We had a couple of days to explore, but it was the beginning of October and we needed to return to Syria before the
winter storms took hold. Our numbers had reduced to ten, the
three who had joined us in Carthage had returned home and
Rob Foote, a friend and one of the ship's committee, had taken
their place. As we sailed out of Malta I got a message from Alice.
She had received a curt email from the Syrian First Lady's secretary telling her that as we had not kept them informed of our
plans for *Phoenicia*'s return to Arwad, there would be no official
reception when we arrived. At the time I was baffled, as Nick
and Alice had been to Syria two months earlier to discuss these
arrangements, but looking back, although the exchanges had
been positive, an ominous silence had followed. Whether we had
unwittingly offended someone or internal political manoeuvring
had been behind their change of heart we would never know.
Whatever had happened the result was the same: there would be
no formal celebration when we returned.

I put it out of my mind and concentrated on our last major
leg. First we had to get to Lebanon, as on our way back to Syria I
had agreed to visit a number of Lebanese ports, where both cultural organisations and individuals had expressed a wish to see
the ship. Once clear of Manoel Island we set an easterly course
for the final thousand miles of our journey. Our progress was
slow, not helped when we ran over a fishing buoy and net during
our first night of sailing. The net tangled itself around the keel
and starboard rudder and we towed the unwelcome hitcher for
several hours before we realised what had happened. As soon as
there was enough light Yuri and Clinton went for a swim so they
could cut the lines free. We may have been coming close to the
end of our journey, but the weather was not going to make it
easy for us and over the next few days we fared little better. For
twenty-four hours the sum of our achievements was to sail in an
elegant but futile figure of eight, only six miles further forward

than we had been the day before. To add to our frustrations the rain began to fall, bringing thunderstorms with it. If that wasn't enough to deal with we were just off a major shipping route, with container vessels passing us frequently, and we had to be constantly alert to the dangers.

Eventually the local depression lifted and the deck began to dry out under the warm Mediterranean sunshine. Life on board followed the same routine except for one new arrival. He had appeared one afternoon, decided he liked his new surroundings and proceeded to make himself comfortable. Our new recruit, whom we named Burt, was a small brown bird and quite un-like the other feathered visitors who had alighted on the ship. Most would stay a few hours before flying off or succumbing to lack of food and exhaustion. We had never been able to per-suade the other birds to eat, not that we had to try in Burt's case. After a good root around he discovered a plentiful supply of cockroaches and other insects and lost no time in hunting them down. Undeterred by the presence of humans, he would fly around the galley with impunity, perching on the kettle handle, coffee cups and computer laptops, even members of the crew. He was last seen one evening on the cabin roof looking out to sea. We hoped he had found another ship to give him refuge or he had summed up enough energy to make it to the nearest land, which was over fifty miles away.

With less than five hundred miles to travel before we reached Lebanon, a glimpse of Crete's mountainous outline came into view. Although the winds picked up and dropped at will we con-tinued to close in on Tyre, the most southerly Phoenician port in Lebanon and our next stop. By 12th October we were near enough to the Israeli coast to see the Golan Heights and, with binoculars, the skyscrapers of Haifa. Occasionally the deafen-ing roar of a military jet would fill the skies above us. As soon as the Israeli navy had picked us up on their radar they made contact with a series of questions. Who were we? What flag were we flying? Where was our intended destination? When were we leaving? Once they were satisfied we posed no threat to them they wished us well and allowed us to continue towards Lebanon. The excitement was growing, we were almost back at our starting point and I began to dare to think about reaching my goal. However, if I thought I had completed the hard task of sailing around Africa and this part would be simple, I had to think again. It was not an auspicious start.

We were looking forward to arriving in Tyre. We knew they were expecting us, and a big celebration had been planned so when we made contact with the Lebanese navy to ask permission to enter their waters we were not anticipating a problem. Our timing could not have been worse. We did not have an appointed shipping agent and, to make matters worse, the Iranian president, Mahmoud Ahmadinejad, was due to visit the following day. His arrival had serious security implications, particularly as he had requested a trip to the south of the country, a Hezbollah stronghold. We were told we would have to remain in international waters and wait for a decision. After sailing around Africa for twenty thousand miles we thought we had experienced every tangled nuance of bureaucracy and the inconvenience that usually followed. We had become philosophical about this sort of delay and viewed it as part of the *Phoenicia* experience. While we waited we spent the time milling around the deck, reading, sleeping or playing cards and chess but the hours ticked by and nothing happened. It was taking so long the crew began to joke we were being held as target practice for the Lebanese warship that had lingered nearby for most of the day. In fact the navy were approachable and professional, on what had been an unusual day for them. I doubted whether a reconstruction of a Phoenician ship had ever attempted to enter one of their most sensitive border ports.

By late afternoon we had still heard nothing and I abandoned hope of getting to our destination. The excitement that had been building among the crew quickly dissipated, and although I maintained radio contact with the navy I set a course for Sidon. We had been sailing for six hours when I got another message from the navy: permission to enter Tyre had been granted and I was told I must go back. By this point we had gone too far and I refused to retrace our track. Although I explained that we were now on our way to Sidon this appeared to make no difference and I was repeatedly ordered to return to Tyre. I stubbornly refused to turn around and, eventually, after protracted discussions, they relented and allowed us to carry on to Sidon.

We arrived as evening fell and were given a berth opposite the 13th century crusader castle that dominated the ancient medieval seaport. Although not quite on the scale of celebrations we had been expecting at Tyre, we received a warm Lebanese welcome from the local officials who were waiting at the quayside. The following day, before a formal celebration at the Bishop of Sidon's palace, we were given a tour of the old city. Sidon has a long history and was one of the oldest Phoenician settlements. Many conquering nations since then have left their mark, including Christian Crusaders and Islamic Mamluks, who shaped most of the medieval walled city. The result is a tangled web of winding alleyways and backstreets, leading to many of Sidon's mosques and churches. As we set off for the tour a motorcade of black limos and outriders roared through the high street, while two Lebanese army helicopters hovered overhead. President Ahmadinejad had arrived in town.

A couple of days later we set sail for Beirut. We left overnight for the twenty-five mile journey up the coast, reaching the main port early the next morning. An official delegation was eagerly awaiting our arrival, and a reception was held alongside the ship with a number of Lebanese cultural organisations in attendance. The Lebanese are fiercely proud of their heritage and they were extremely grateful that we were trying to highlight the achievements of their forebears.

It was wonderful to have official recognition of the expedition's success, but shortly after we arrived our celebrations were tempered by bad news. Aziz had received a message from home and was in a distressed state when he found me.

'I need to fly back to Jakarta. My father has died and I must return for his funeral,' he explained, as he fought back the tears.

I arranged his flight and he left immediately. It was a devastating blow for him and a terrible way to end his time on *Phoenicia*. At times we had clashed as he passionately defended his beliefs, but he had been one of my most dependable crew and I would miss his directness and honesty. He had got so close to seeing the journey through to the end and bringing *Phoenicia* home to Arwad and I felt for him. It was an emotional farewell for those who had travelled with him for months, particularly Sulhan and Dirman.

As our thoughts turned to our final destination we received an invitation from officials in Tripoli asking us if we would pay them a visit. This had been another important Phoenician city, forming the centre of an alliance between Sidon, Tyre and Arwad, and it was on our route home. We gratefully accepted, knowing it was going to be the last official celebration of the expedition. We could never have imagined we would get such a spectacular welcome.

It was a warm, clear morning as we approached Tripoli's port of El Mina. News of our visit had spread and fishing vessels began to gather in the water around us. As we got closer to the jetty we were stunned by the sight that came into view: two thousand people had packed the quayside to welcome us, all of them cheering and shouting. Hundreds of children were jumping up, craning to get a glimpse of the ship, while waving flags and screaming with delight. On both sides of the jetty musicians robed in traditional gold and black costumes had lined up to greet us, and as the drums beat out a rhythm dancers began to sway. It was as if we had arrived at a festival and the exuberance of the crowd was infectious. *Phoenicia* was draped in flags, while lifeguards had to prevent enthusiastic crowds trying to scramble on board. As we made it onto the jetty we were covered with garlands of flowers and welcomed by our hosts. Reporters and television crews swarmed around us, keen to know what it was like to sail on board a Phoenician ship and what had been the highlights and low points of our long journey. When the interviews were over we were taken to a reception at the Mayor's office, followed by a lunch with the President of the Cultural Committee of Tripoli. They thanked us for reviving the Phoenicians' great heritage in shipbuilding and sea trade and for bringing to greater prominence their contribution to world history.

The day concluded with a formal evening reception, after which dancers and drummers escorted us back to the ship. We were reluctant for the party to end and the crew continued to dance on deck, tired, ecstatic and bowled over by our warm and enthusiastic welcome. On our last day, while local schools came to visit the ship, some of us were given a tour of the ancient Phoenician ports of Bartroum and Byblos. I gave a final presentation on the background to the expedition, our journey and what came next. By now my thoughts were turning to the future of the *Phoenicia* project.

We were ready for the final leg and there was a sense of euphoria as we neared the end of our journey. This was the last opportunity for people to take part in the expedition and we had five more recruits keen to take part. Two had not sailed with us before: Victoria Sadler was a member of the ship's committee whose son, Edward, had been sailing with us since the Azores, and Mohamad Osman was a Syrian shipping owner who had been a generous sponsor. Another Syrian, Karim Khwanda, had participated in the leg to Cape Town and wanted to see *Phoenicia* return to his homeland. Nick Swallow came back for the third time and Alice left the office to join us. I was glad that after all her hard work she would be on board *Phoenicia* for the final leg. It was a multinational crew, as it had been throughout the journey.

We had revelled in the celebrations in Lebanon knowing we would be sailing quietly into Arwad, but we had not considered the impact our arrival in Lebanon was having on her neighbour. The rivalry between the two countries was intense and it prompted a rapid change of heart by the Syrian authorities. Syria would not be outdone; if Lebanon were celebrating our achievements they would have to do the same. Forty-eight hours before we arrived we were told to expect an official welcome for *Phoenicia*'s homecoming.

It was a small distance to sail and having set out at nine in the evening we were within sight of Arwad by the early hours of the following morning. A few miles from our destination we stopped, cleared immigration and customs and waited for the order to proceed. There was a huge sense of anticipation on board. Some were excited to be close to the end of their journey, while others seemed to be in a more reflective mood, perhaps contemplating the final time they would stand on her deck.

Alice looked at me and smiled, 'You've done it Philip. *Phoenicia* has made it back.'

It was 23rd October 2010, two years and two months since I had last seen the little island of Arwad. It had taken six years from the first idea to this moment and now the culmination of all our hard work was in front of us.

At ten o'clock we began our approach. Fishing boats, coastguard vessels and tugs came out to meet us until we were surrounded by more than fifty, each one packed with people waving and shouting. An official party of dignitaries joined us on board for the final mile of our journey. When we got closer we began to hear waves of chanting coming from the island. Marine flares hissed as orange smoke billowed into the sky, and when the crowds came into view the noise reached a deafening pitch, as the shouting, chanting and clapping continued. Without a word Clinton scrambled to the top of the mast and stood on the yardarm waving a Syrian flag. Suddenly everyone on board began to cheer and hug each other as the excitement from the quay washed over us. It was too much for Sulhan. Perhaps there had been times he had wondered if we would ever make it back; overcome with emotion he fell to the deck and prayed, tears streaming down his face.

We disembarked and made our way along the jetty, through a riot of noise and colour. Hundreds of islanders, press and invited guests did their best to jostle for space on the small quay. It was chaos but the most enthusiastic and joyful chaos any of us could have imagined. Among the crowd I could make out some familiar faces. Orwah and his father were shouting and waving, while Khalid just beamed with pride. A line of official dignitaries came forward to speak, welcoming *Phoenicia* and her crew back to Arwad and congratulating us on the success of our project. It was a hero's welcome, worthy of the Phoenician sailors who had taken the first epic voyage, and an emotional moment for everyone involved in the project. By late afternoon the press interviews were over, the celebrations had died down and the crowds had dispersed. We sailed *Phoenicia* over to the mainland with the British ambassador and other officials on board. There the party continued with a gala dinner and more presentations and accolades to mark our achievement. We discovered we had been the first news item on Syrian state television that evening. Later we learned it was unprecedented for an event like ours to be the lead news story.

The following day the crew had a well-deserved rest. Some spent time with their families, who had flown out to be with them, while others began making plans to leave. Although Clinton disappeared without a word the rest of us met up in the evening for one final meal. The expedition was over and our time together was coming to an end, but I hoped those who had taken part felt they had achieved their own personal goals. We had shared *Phoenicia*'s difficulties and triumphs and I think most of us had been changed by the experience.

The next few days went quickly. A handful of crew – Rob, Steph, Dirman and Sulhan – remained behind to help me and we sailed *Phoenicia* back to Arwad. We stored the sails and ropes and bagged up a considerable amount of leftover tinned food, which was distributed among the poorest families on the island. Meanwhile Orwah was delighted to get a very good deal on a powerful jet ski.

It was a strange feeling as I watched Phoenicia being pulled up onto dry dock. She had been an almost constant companion for two years and although I was relieved the voyage was over, it was a wrench leaving her behind. I said goodbye to Orwah and Khalid and told them I would return in a few months. As we made our way back to the mainland the final members of crew dispersed and Dirman said goodbye, still smiling as broadly as he had done on the day of his arrival in Aden many months before.

While I was preparing to leave I got a message from the First Lady's office inviting the crew to come to see her. By this time everyone had gone so I went alone. During our meeting she was surprisingly enthusiastic about the expedition. I discussed *Phoenicia*'s future with her and my intention to set up a foundation. I wanted to use the ship to teach young people about Phoenician history and culture, and to give some the opportunity to take part in short voyages, allowing them to get a taste of the *Phoenicia* experience. I hoped that learning the technical skills and challenges of sailing an ancient ship would foster a spirit of adventure in others and inspire them to want to explore. She seemed taken by the idea, although by now I was wary of any pledge of endorsement. During our meeting there was no mention or explanation of why she had withdrawn her support so abruptly, but ultimately it had made no difference; *Phoenicia* had successfully circumnavigated Africa and I had achieved what I had set out to do.

I had wanted to recreate what I believed to be one of the greatest and most daring maritime voyages in history, but in the process the Phoenicians had taught me far more than just their seafaring skills. I had gained an immense respect for their courage and tenacity. They would not be limited by the beliefs of their time and, undeterred by the dangers, they ventured out through waters thought too dangerous to sail, conquering man's natural fear of the unknown in their pursuit of greater knowledge. By testing the limits of a Phoenician ship I had tested my own limits. The expedition had come close to failure many times: we had run the gauntlet of pirate-infested waters, overcome numerous technical problems and travelled deep into the Indian and Atlantic Oceans. She had been a difficult ship to sail but we had learnt by trial and error. I had proved she was an ocean-going vessel and when she was coasting along the waves, her sail billowing in the wind, to captain her had been an unforgettable experience.

I had begun the expedition believing the Phoenicians had been the first to circumnavigate Africa and I returned even more convinced of this fact. I hope that one day evidence will come to light that will settle the matter conclusively. Until then I will continue to dream, follow my convictions and explore.

All men dream: but not equally. Those who dream by night in the dusty recesses of their minds wake in the day to find that it was vanity: but the dreamers of the day are dangerous men, for they may act their dream with open eyes, to make it possible.

T. E. Lawrence,
Seven Pillars of Wisdom

Postscript

In 2011 the Arab Spring began to change the political map of the Middle East, and by March of that year Syria had become embroiled in her own internal struggles. A brutal crackdown by government forces and retaliation by pro-democracy supporters has brought the country to the brink of civil war. As the situation deteriorated plans for a foundation in Syria began to look increasingly unlikely, and by June I realised it was no longer possible to leave *Phoenicia* in Arwad. Orwah, Khalid and the other islanders rely on fishing and tourism for their survival and they face a desperate and uncertain future. It was a sad departure and all those involved in the *Phoenicia* project wish them well.

Over four months *Phoenicia* was moved to a number of Mediterranean ports, and in the spring of 2012 a small crew and I sailed her back to the UK, where she was opened to the public at St Katharine Docks, London. An exhibition on board shows her amazing journey and the history of the seafarers who first took similar ships to the oceans. I hope in this way she will inspire others and we can continue the legacy of the Phoenicia Expedition.

The Azores Question Revisited

In March 2012 I came across a fascinating research project, which appeared to shed further light on the Azores question. Three members of the Portuguese Association for Archaeological Investigation, Nuno Ribeiro, Anabela Joaquinito and Sergio Pereira, presented data they had collected from two islands in the Azores: Corvo and Terceira. During their investigations they discovered a number of sites where underground chambers had been excavated into the soft volcanic rock. They varied in size but some were very large, reaching up to a hundred and eighty metres deep and a hundred and sixty metres high; others were still sealed by small blocks of stone. Inside there appeared to be carved altar-like structures, troughs and several post holes.

Although more work needs to be done, Nuno Ribeiro described these finds to me as 'irrefutable evidence' of the existence of a pre-Christian occupation of the Azores. These chambers show striking similarities to a number of Iron Age sites found in the Mediterranean region, corresponding to the time of the Etruscan, Hellenic, Egyptian and Phoenician cultures. Given the Phoenicians were expert seafarers and had colonies in the Canary Islands and along the Atlantic coast of North Africa, the available evidence would seem to suggest that they were the most likely to have discovered the Azores. In fact these Portuguese archaeologists strongly believe the structures they found represent 4th century BC Carthaginian temples. If this assessment were correct it would confirm my theory that the Phoenicians used the islands as a staging post when returning to the Mediterranean from their African colonies. It would also explain how the Phoenicians could have circumnavigated Africa from east to west without staying close to the coast.

If the Phoenicians knew of the Azores then tales from the first Portuguese explorers can no longer be dismissed as mere myth. This, in turn, would raise the question that if the man sitting on a stone horse was more than just a legend, does a finger pointing across the Atlantic hint at another epic seafaring journey? It is possible that this ancient civilisation has one more incredible maritime story and perhaps *Phoenicia* and I will take to the seas again to tell it one day.

Acknowledgements

This project would not have been possible without the hard work, enthusiasm and generosity of others, their contribution was immeasurable. I would like to thank the following:

Core Crew

Niklas Andersson (*Sweden*), Abdul Aziz (*Indonesia*), John Bainbridge (*UK*), Alice Chutter (*UK*), Clinton Clements (*South Africa*), Danielle Eubank (*USA*), Steph Edwards (*UK),* Rob Foote (*UK*), Daniel Hallstrom (*USA*), Dirman Sahadan Haruna (*Indonesia*), Len Helfrich (*South Africa*), Eric Hebert (*Canada*), Peter Hickman (*South Africa*), Sulhan Jawani Nasir (*Indonesia*), Alice Palmer (*USA*), Edward Sadler (*UK*), Vera Sanada (*Brazil*), Yuri Sanada (*Brazil*), Nicolas Swallow (*UK)*

Additional Crew

Adnan Attia (*Syria*), Khalifa Alzaabi (*Oman*), Warren Aston (*Australia*), Youssof Al-Agbri (Oman), Ali Al-Balushi (*Oman*), Justin Bean (*South Africa*), Karen Bowerman (*UK*), Rebecca Delmar-Morgan (*UK*), Nigel Fransham (*UK*), John Glenister (*South Africa*), Rashid Al Ghuzaili (*Oman*), Vanessa Hickman (*South Africa*), John Horseman (*UK*), Merryn Johnson (*UK*), Keith Johnson (*USA*), Amin Kanafani (*Syria*), Richard Kellie (*Canada*), Karim Khwanda (*Syria*), Salah Al-Khatri (*Oman*), Tony Lambdon (*NZ*), Natalie Lumby (*UK*), Jev Mavksimovs (*Latvia*), Colin Moore (*UK*), Robert Onion (*UK*), Mohamad Osman (*Syria*), Hisham Abdul Razzak (*Syria*), Julia Rous (*UK*), Paul Reid (*USA*), Suhra (*Indonesia*), Victoria Sadler (*UK*), Atsuko Senno (*Japan*), Doug Smith (*UK*), Kim Vickers (*UK*), Mike Wilcox (*UK*).

Ship's Committee & Management Team

Paul Bayly, Alice Chutter, Rob Foote, Eric Hebert, Reg Hill, Laurenne Mansbridge, Victoria Sadler, Lauren Simpson, Doug Smith, Nicolas Swallow (chairman), Sarah Taylor, Gordon Teenan, Kim Vickers

Technical

Nick Burningham, Kostas Damianidis, Harry Tzalas

Academic

(Dr) Lucy Blue, (Professor) Barry Cunlile, Honor Frost, (Professor) Sean McGrail, (Professor) Patrice Pomey, Jonathan Tubb, (Dr) Julian Whitewright

Supporters, partners, friends and advisers

El-Lamei Adel Abdou, – *Mitchell Junior,* Muhammad Abu Bakker – *Arwad, Syria,* Orwah Abu Bakker – *Arwad, Syria,* (Dr) Fawaz Akhraz, (Dr) Khair

Al-Din Al-Sayed – *Tartous Health Authority,* Azm and Saadeh Organization
- *Tripoli, Lebanon,* Antoine Menassa – *Franco Lebanese Cultural Centre, Paris,*
Barney Broom – *Film maker/presenter,* Chris Baker – *Fischer Panda,* (Captain)
Bassam – *Maritime A!airs Authority, Yemen,* Mark Baum"eld – *British Council,*
Imad Bitar – *Orient Bridge Group,* Ramic Bitar – *Orient Bridge Group,* Karen
Bowerman – *Film maker/presenter,* British Lebanese Society, British Museum,
British Syrian Society, Malika Brown – *Freelance journalist,* Philip Browning –
Articulate, Caroline Cecil – *Caroline Cecil Associates,* Samer Dabliz – *Coordinator
Lebanon,* Paul Docksey – *Artist & sculptor,* Paul Doubleday – *British Council,*
Dougie Douglas – *Etihad, Jakarta,* Jack Draper – *Woodworker,* Mohamed
A Emara – *Suez Canal Authority,* Danielle Eubank – *Artist,* Anne Evans
– *HTI,* George Faddoul – *Co-ordinator Lebanon,* Krystal Fiksdal – *MBI Al
Jaber Foundation,* Emile Foote – *Private supporter,* Liz Formby – *HTI,* Alaa
Ghandoura – *Ghandoura Group,* Mohamad Ghandoura – *Ghandoura Group,*
Nadim Ghantous – *Arab Bank Lebanon,* Ian & Jean Gillespie – *Private
supporters,* Lance Godefroy – *Navionics,* Alex Goodey – *Media specialist,* Simon
Greenly – *Greenlys Holdings,* Bob Haddow – *Drum Cussac,* Sasha Hafez –
Orient Bridge Group, Mustafa Hamadeh – *Private supporter,* Abou Hammoud –
Shipwright, Khaled Hammoud – *Shipwright,* Fouad Hannoun – *Arabia Insurance,*
Mark Harriman – *Viking Life Saving Equipment,* Martin Hesp – *Journalist,*
Rosemary Hodder – *Private supporter,* John Horseman – *Private supporter,* (Dr)
Sean Hudson – *Founder, Expedition Medicine,* Alyemany Khaled Hussain –
Embassy of the Republic of Yemen, Nelly Hussaini, – *Lions Club, Lebanon,* Nick
Farrell – *Yellow Brick Adventure Tracking,* Rosie, Andy & Merryn Johnson –
Private Supporters, Joana Kalkali – *Byblos Bank (Syria),* Fares Kallas – *Damascus,
Syria,* (Captain) Hamza Kanafani – *Tartous, Syria,* (Captain) Mustafa Kanafani
– *IMO Syria,* (Dr). Hanan Kassab-Hassan – *Secretary General, Damascus 2008,*
Salim George Khalaf – *Phoenicia International Research Centre,* The Lebanese
Cultural Union, (Dr) Keek – *Deputy Mayor, Tripoli Lebanon,* The Safadi
Foundation - *Tripoli Lebanon,* (Dr) Sami Khiyami – *Damascus,Syria,* Ibtissam
Khoury – *Co-ordinator Lebanon,* Karim Khwanda – *Damascus, Syria,* Roger King
– *Drum Cussac,* Hassan Kraytem – *Beruit Port,* Hazem Dwik – *Arabia Insurance,*
Naquib Latif – *Felix Shipping Agents,* Claire Livesey – *Circle,* Sue Losson –
Green People, Radwan Loutfi – *Minister Plenipotentiary,* Hugh and Natalie Lumby
– *Private supporters,* Jihad Makdissi – *Damascus, Syria,* Laurenne Mansbridge
– *Pioneer Expeditions,* Colin Moore – *Artist,* Dugal Muller – *Private supporter,*
Terry Newberry – *Private supporter,* Robert Onion – *Circle,* Claire Osborne
– *Whale Pumps,* Mohamad Osman – *Osman Shipping LLC,* Fiona Pankhurst –
Raymarine, Jo Phillip – *Independent PR advisor,* Lilas Rabbat – *Damascus, Syria,*
Charles Ramseyer – *SoCal,* Raphael & Nicky Ravenscroft – *Private Supporters,*
Mark Redwood – *Private supporter,* John Roberts – *Aqualuce,* Eugene L Rogan

– *The Middle East Centre, Oxford University,* Abdul Kader Sabra – *Federation of Syrian Shipping,* Ric Searle – *Yellow Brick Adventure Tracking,* Adnan Shaban – *Damascus, Syria,* Rita Smith – *Language Centre Publications,* Farquhar Sterling – *Private supporter,* Thompson's Gallery – *London,* Laura Trant – *BBC South,* Themis Violaris – *Monarch Telecom,* Lily Wardoyo – *Private supporter,* (Captain) Wasim – *Marina Saint George, Beirut, Lebanon,* Jim Watkins – *Private Supporter,* William Weld – *Private Supporter,* David Wickham – *Independent Image,* Stephan Wickham – *Independent Image,* Shane Windser – *Royal Geographical Society,* Rawa Younes – *Syrian Air*

Sponsors

Aventura, Aqualuce, Arabia Insurance, Axis House, Byblos Bank – Syria, Circle,

Delheim Wines, Fisher Panda, Global Freight Solutions, LCP, Navionics, Ocean Services – Alexandria, Ocean Village – Gibraltar, Osman Shipping LLC, Pioneer Expeditions, Raymarine, SoCal, Syrian Chamber of Shipping, Viking Life Support Equipment, Whale marine pumps, Yellow Brick

Ports, Marinas and Yacht Clubs

Algoa Bay Yacht Club, Port Elizabeth, South Africa

Horta Marina, Horta, Azores

Island of Arwad , Syria

Manoel Island Yacht Marina

Marina Saint George, Beirut Lebanon

Maritime A!airs Authority, Yemen

Mayotte Yacht Club, Mayotte

Ocean Village Marina, Gibraltar

Point Yacht Club, Durban, South Africa

Port of Tartous, Syria

Ports of Beirut, Sidon and Tripoli, Lebanon

Royal Cape Yacht Club , South Africa

Royal Natal Yacht Club, Durban, South Africa

Saint Helena Yacht Club

V&A Waterfront, Cape Town

Zululand Yacht Club, Richards Bay, South Africa

Photo credits

Front cover photograph: Danielle Eubank (www.danielleeubank.com). Other photographs copyright of the Phoenicia Ship Expedition and courtesy of Danielle Eubank, Eric Hebert, John Bainbridge, Abdul Aziz, Steph Edwards, Niklas Andersson, Yuri Sanada, Jennie Hill, Carl and Rachel Severson.

References

Chapter 1
[1] De Sélincourt, A. *Herodotus: The Histories*, Harmondsworth: Penguin, 1954; p. 255. Out of print.

Chapter 9
[1] The Fitzwilliam Museum *What does Kemet mean?* [online] Available from: http://www.fitzmuseum.cam.ac.uk/dept/ant/egypt/kemet/virtualkemet/faq [Accessed 10/02/12]

Chapter 18
[1] Armstrong, P. H. *A Rock and a Cinder: St Helena and Ascension. In Darwin's Other Islands*, New York: Continuum, 2004; p.229.
[2] Yapp, P. (Ed). *The Travellers' Dictionary of Quotation: who said what, about where?*, London: Routledge, 1983; p.16.

Chapter 20
[1] Archaeology: Before Columbus or the Vikings. *Time Magazine* 1968, May 24th.
[2] Bikai, Patricia M. and Pierre M. Timelines: A Phoenician Fable. *Archaeology* 1990, January / February.

Chapter 21
[1] Rawlinson, G. *Phoenicia: History of a Civilisation*, London: I.B. Tauris, 2005; p.70.

Chapter 22
[1] Aubet, M.E. *The Phoenicians and the West: politics, colonies and trade* 2nd edition, Cambridge: Cambridge University Press, 2001; p.280.
[2] Herm, G. *The Phoenicians: the Purple Empire of the Ancient World.* New York: Morrow, 1975; p.202.

Chapter 23
[1] Fantar, M'hamed Hassine. *Carthage: The Punic City Collection Mediterranean Heritage,* Tunisia, 2007; p.8.
[2] Aubet, M.E. *The Phoenicians and the West: politics, colonies and trade* 2nd edition, Cambridge: Cambridge University Press, 2001; p.175.

Chapter 24
[1] Castillo, D.A. *The Maltese Cross: A strategic history of Malta,* Westport, CT: Praeger, 2006; p.52.
[2] Bonnici, J, Cassar, M. *A Chronicle of Twentieth Century Malta,* Malta: Book Distributors Ltd, 2004; p.296.
[3] Duclos, A. *Cippus from Malta* [online] Department of Near Eastern Antiquities: Levant, Louvre. Available from: http://www.louvre.fr/en/oeuvre-notices/cippus-malta [Accessed 20/03/12]
[4] Avasthi, A. *Phoenician Blood Endures 3,000 years, DNA Study Shows* [online] Available from: http://news.nationalgeographic.com/news/2008/10/081030-phoenician-dna-genographic-missions. html [Accessed 15/01/12]

Bibliography

Alpozen, T. Oguz, Ozdas A Harun, and Bahadir Berkaya. *Commercial amphoras of the Bodrum Museum of Underwater Archaeology: maritime trade of the Mediterranean in ancient times.* Bodrum, Turkey: Bodrum Museum of Underwater Archaeology, 1995. Print.

Aubet, Maria Eugenia. *The Phoenicians and the West: politics, colonies, and trade.* Cambridge, England: Cambridge University Press, 1993. Print.

Bass, George Fletcher. *A history of seafaring; based on underwater archaeology.* New York: Walker, 1972. Print.

Bass, George Fletcher. *A history of seafaring; based on underwater archaeology.* New York: Walker, 1972. Print.

Casson, Lionel. *Ships and seamanship in the ancient world.* Princeton, N.J.: Princeton University Press, 1971. Print.

Casson, Lionel. *The ancient mariners: seafarers and sea fighters of the Mediterranean in ancient times.* 2nd ed. Princeton, N.J.: Princeton University Press, 1991. Print.

Cunliffe, Barry W. *Europe between the oceans: themes and variations, 9000 BC - AD 1000.* New Haven: Yale University Press, 2008. Print.

Fantar, M'hamed Hassine. *Carthage: The Punic City Collection Mediterranean Heritage,* English Edition, Tunisia,2007. Print.

Gibbons, Tony. *The encyclopedia of ships.* San Diego, CA: Thunder Bay Press, 2001. Print.

Harden, Donald B. *The Phoenicians.* New York: Praeger, 1962. Print.

Herm, Gerhard. *The Phoenicians: the Purple Empire of the ancient world.* New York: Morrow, 1975. Print.

Holst, Sanford. *Phoenician secrets: exploring the ancient Mediterranean.* Los Angeles, California. Santorini Books, 2011. Print.

Jenkins, Nancy, and Ahmed Youssef Moustafa. *The boat beneath the pyramid: King Cheops' royal ship.* New York: Holt, Rinehart and Winston, 1980. Print.

Markoe, Glenn. *Phoenicians.* Berkeley: University of California Press, 2000. Print.

Marston, Elsa. *Phoenicians.* New York: Benchmark Books/Marshall Cavendish, 2002. Print.

McGrail, Sean. *Boats of the world: from the Stone Age to Medieval times.* Oxford: Oxford University Press, 2002. Print.

Miles, Richard. *Carthage must be destroyed: the rise and fall of an ancient civilization.* New York: Viking, 2011. Print.

Moscati, Sabatino. *The Phoenicians.* New York: Abbeville Press, 1988. Print.

Picard, Gilbert and Colette Picard. *The life and death of Carthage; a survey of Punic history and culture from its birth to the final tragedy.* New York: Taplinger Pub. Co. 1969. Print.

Pudney, John. *Suez; De Lesseps' canal.* New York: Praeger, 1969. Print.

Ribeiro, Nuno et al. Phoenicians in the Azores, Myth or Reality? *The fifteenth annual symposium on Mediterranean Archaeology (SOMA) Catania, March 2011.* Unpublished.

Rawlinson, George. *History of Phoenicia.* London: Longmans, Green, 1889. Print.

Synge, M. B. *A book of discovery.* New ed. London: Nelson, 1962. Print.

Tubb, Jonathan N. *Canaanites.* Norman: University of Oklahoma Press, 1998. Print.

Waddell, L. A. *The Indo-Sumerian seals deciphered, discovering Sumerians of Indus valley as Phoenicians, Barats, Goths & famous Vedic Aryans, 3100-2300 B.C.* London: Luzac & Co., 1925. Print.

Waterfield, Robin and Carolyn Dewald. *The histories.* Oxford, Oxford University Press, 1998. Print.

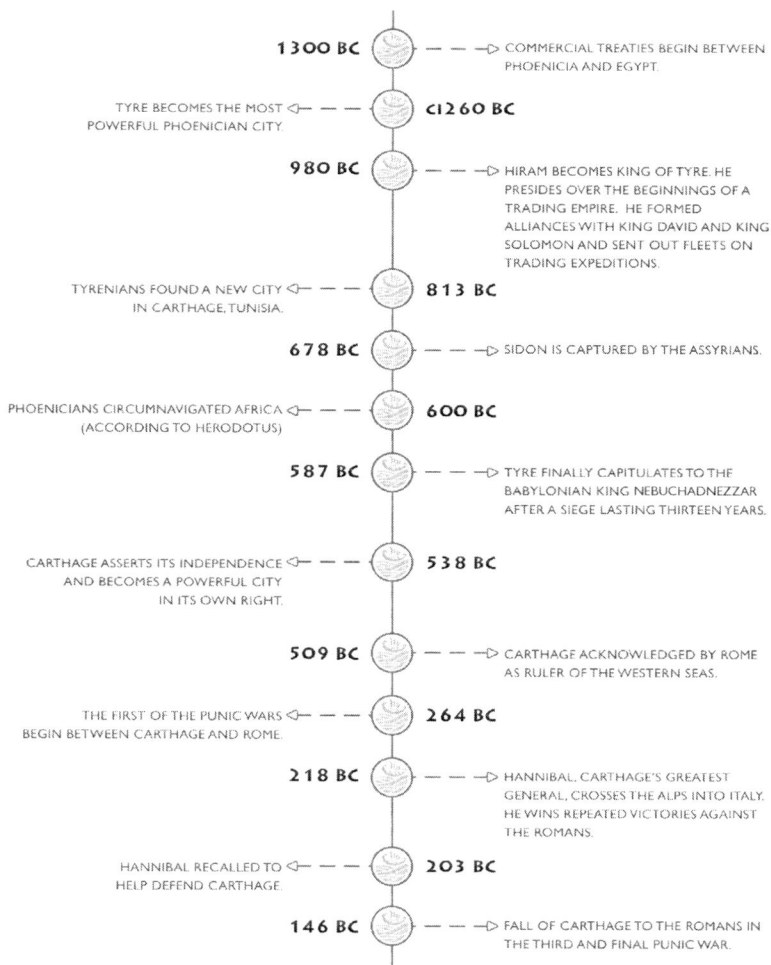

TIMELINE

1300 BC — — —▷ COMMERCIAL TREATIES BEGIN BETWEEN PHOENICIA AND EGYPT.

TYRE BECOMES THE MOST ◁— — — **C1260 BC**
POWERFUL PHOENICIAN CITY.

980 BC — — —▷ HIRAM BECOMES KING OF TYRE. HE PRESIDES OVER THE BEGINNINGS OF A TRADING EMPIRE. HE FORMED ALLIANCES WITH KING DAVID AND KING SOLOMON AND SENT OUT FLEETS ON TRADING EXPEDITIONS.

TYRENIANS FOUND A NEW CITY ◁— — — **813 BC**
IN CARTHAGE, TUNISIA.

678 BC — — —▷ SIDON IS CAPTURED BY THE ASSYRIANS.

PHOENICIANS CIRCUMNAVIGATED AFRICA ◁— — — **600 BC**
(ACCORDING TO HERODOTUS)

587 BC — — —▷ TYRE FINALLY CAPITULATES TO THE BABYLONIAN KING NEBUCHADNEZZAR AFTER A SIEGE LASTING THIRTEEN YEARS.

CARTHAGE ASSERTS ITS INDEPENDENCE ◁— — — **538 BC**
AND BECOMES A POWERFUL CITY
IN ITS OWN RIGHT.

509 BC — — —▷ CARTHAGE ACKNOWLEDGED BY ROME AS RULER OF THE WESTERN SEAS.

THE FIRST OF THE PUNIC WARS ◁— — — **264 BC**
BEGIN BETWEEN CARTHAGE AND ROME.

218 BC — — —▷ HANNIBAL, CARTHAGE'S GREATEST GENERAL, CROSSES THE ALPS INTO ITALY. HE WINS REPEATED VICTORIES AGAINST THE ROMANS.

HANNIBAL RECALLED TO ◁— — — **203 BC**
HELP DEFEND CARTHAGE.

146 BC — — —▷ FALL OF CARTHAGE TO THE ROMANS IN THE THIRD AND FINAL PUNIC WAR.

Facts and figures

Length of journey	over 20,000 miles
Ports of call	24
Countries and territories visited	15
Number of crew	53 from 14 countries
Phoenicia's fastest recorded speed	10.6 knots (with strong current off the Wild Coast, South Africa)
Longest leg	84 days at sea from Ascension Island to the Azores
Smallest number of crew on a single leg	6
Largest number of crew on a single leg	15
Longest port stop	Port Sudan 10 weeks
Amount of rope used for the rigging	380m
Weight of yard and sail	1000kg
Weight of anchor and chain	350kg
Length of longest anchor chain	40m
Number of anchors taken on voyage	5